Africa and the West

JERAH JOHNSON
University of New Orleans

The Dryden Press
901 North Elm Street
Hinsdale, Illinois 60521

Preface

This little book developed out of almost two decades of experience teaching western-civilization courses in large state universities in the South. Over the years I became increasingly concerned with two problems. The first was the ever more apparent need to enlarge our conception of western civilization to take account of some of its non-European components. The other was how to make courses in western civilization relevant to black students, a problem that grew more pressing, it seemed to me, as separatist movements developed in the black community.

Whether writing from a European or an American vantage point, historians have, almost without exception, envisaged western civilization as a complex progression traceable from ancient Egyptian, Mesopotamian, Greek, and Roman origins through the Medieval centuries and the age of discovery to the development of the New World and Modern Europe. Though this outline has been convenient and useful, it is proving not only limiting but also misleading. Historians have, during recent years, drawn attention to defects in the accepted historical panorama of western civilization, and their efforts have resulted in some alterations. An increasing number of scholars today are producing specialized studies extending the conception of western civilization; some textbook writers, meanwhile, have responded to this challenge by including chapters on the Moslem world, the Byzantine Empire, Indian history, and the Far East in their surveys of western history. This expanded perspective is surely necessary to classify our past and to provide a better perspective for projection of our future. But one glaring distortion still remains in the Western panorama.

Black Africa has largely escaped notice. The work of African specialists, both those writing on present-day affairs and those reconstructing the early history of the continent, appeals to only a small audience. Other historians who treat black Africa at all do so in a limited way. Europeans writing on Africa restrict themselves, for the most part, to nineteenth-century imperialism and its twentieth-century aftermath, while American historians who have lately developed an interest in the Negro in the New World concern themselves only incidentally with his African background. And western civilization textbook writers have generally ignored black Africa altogether. There has been, in short, little attempt, outside of a handful of black American scholars, to relate black Africa to the course of western development.

As I puzzled over all this, the solution to my second problem, that of making western civilization meaningful to black American students, suddenly struck me. In Africa lay the answer. The simple truth was that, far from being outside the western tradition, American blacks were central to its historical development. Europeans pushed across the Atlantic and discovered the Americas, but they could not develop the new found lands. They lacked the manpower. Much of that had to come from black Africa, and it came in the form of slave labor. Black Africa thus became a vital and necessary part of expanding western civilization.

The essay that follows is an effort to treat European and African history together, to view the histories of the two continents, along with the opening of the Atlantic, as the basic components of western civilization. Given the present state of our knowledge, such an attempt can be only provisional—or better, a plea for further inquiry and discussion. At this time we know very little about ancient Africa; many aspects of medieval and early-modern slavery remain unexplored; the role of the Negro in the making of America is just beginning to be studied; and early relationships between Africa and Europe have hardly been touched. In spite of such deficiencies, the present effort is prompted by a felt need to get before readers something of what we already know about these questions, thereby providing an alternative framework for a somewhat different way of examining the development of western civilization, and, at the same time, to chart some avenues for further study.

In attempting to view the two continents together in historical perspective, I have been forced to retell, to a certain extent, the story of each. In the retelling I have sought not to repeat, for Europe at least, the already familiar political narrative or to sketch again old faces. Instead I have tried to provide the reader with information on the fundamentals of civilization development—peoples, settlement patterns, labor, agriculture, trade, and the arts. For Africa, about which considerably less is generally known by readers, I have felt it important to include more on both politics and personalities though, there too, most of the attention is given to the more important, if mundane, cultural developments.

The present essay reflects little in the way of original or archival research. Instead it is an attempt to draw together into some kind of meaningful synthesis what we already know about Europe, Africa, and the Americas. The audience for whom I have written is not primarily the specialist though I naturally hope that he might find the work of some interest, but the teachers and students, as well as those among the general public, who might feel the need to know something more about the historic interplay between blacks and whites and the role of each in the formative stages of what has been called, in our own day, an Atlantic civilization. The work seems particularly timely to me as an antidote to the increasingly heard contention from black separatists (and an alarming number of their white supporters) that blacks have no part in western civilization. Hopefully this little book might help to counteract that view.

In a book this short on a subject this large, problems of conflicting interpretations are met on almost every page, if not in almost every paragraph. I have called the reader's attention to differing interpretations when it seemed important to do so; otherwise I have simply chosen and woven into the narrative the particular interpretations that I found most convincing. Similarly, the book was written without footnotes, for it seemed to me that for most readers notes are neither necessary nor useful. The bibliographic essay at the end of the volume provides information on differing interpretations of key issues in the narrative as well as a guide for further reading.

Writing this essay has afforded me the pleasure not only of reading widely in fields of scholarship other than my own, but of discussing aspects of the subject with many friends and colleagues. These discussions have clarified many points for me and saved me from many errors, though, needless to say, whatever inaccuracies remain are entirely my responsibility. The debt I owe is so great that I can record here only a fraction of it. For typing the manuscript I owe more than I can ever repay to the patience and skill of Mrs. Nita Walsh; and to two graduate assistants, Cintra S. Austin and James Albins, I owe almost as much. David and Bonnie Bergeron, George G. Windell, William A. Percy, William Savage, and Stephen E. Ambrose have read all or portions of the manuscript and given me the benefit of their keen critical faculties. Gordon Mueller's and Joseph Logsdon's reading of the whole led me to make important substantive changes. The latter's constant interest, encouragement, and suggestions, from the inception of the idea to the completion of the essay, have been a sustaining force. And to the advisory editor of the press, Professor Keith W. Eubank, I wish to express particular appreciation. He recognized merit in the project early on, and gave generously of his time and editorial acumen, a factor that accounts, in a large way, for its fruition. I thank them all.

New Orleans
Summer, 1973
                                              Jerah Johnson

Contents

CHAPTER ONE

Europe, Africa, and the Mediterranean: An Introduction

Before astronaut Neil Armstrong set foot on the moon, the most momentous event in history was the trans-Atlantic voyage of Christopher Columbus. Of almost unimaginable daring within itself, Columbus's act quite literally and instantaneously doubled the size of the world known to Europeans and simultaneously initiated an unparalleled enlargement of the scope of western civilization. Not only would the Americas, north and south, become major stockholders in an enlarged western civilization as it spread to their shores and penetrated their hinterlands, but black Africans, by virtue of their crucial role as the slave-labor force that developed the New World, could also claim a share.

If asked to trace the evolving course of Western civilization on a map, most people, guided by what they recalled from textbooks, would probably draw a broad line from the eastern Mediterranean through Greece, on across to Italy—that is to say, Rome—then up through the river valleys of France and southern Germany to western Europe, and thence across the Atlantic to the New World. There the line would end. Such a charting, indeed, is the line along which western civilization is traditionally said to have traveled. But such a course is only a half reckoning. A complementary line, perhaps not quite so broad but nonetheless distinct, should be drawn from the same point of origin in the eastern Mediterranean through Greece and Rome, but then down across the Sahara to the interior of black Africa, thence westward to the Guinea Coast, and from there across the Atlantic to the Americas where it would intersect the first line. The progress of what we today know as western civilization was along both routes.

The lines on our map diverge widely, one encompassing much of Europe and the other a large part of Africa. But they have a common point of origin, the Mediterranean. That sea and the culture that developed around it in ancient times was the initial point of contact between the European and African worlds. The Mediterranean itself was more of a bond than a barrier between the two worlds, for both Africa and Europe were oriented to it for much of their histories.

Each continent developed more or less independently and in isolation for the first several thousand years of its history. Not until the Romans conquered virtually the entire known world and penetrated the Sahara were black Africa and Europe able to begin any meaningful contacts with one another. But hardly had that process got underway when the Roman imperium collapsed, bringing to an end the ancient Mediterranean civilization that had been the meeting ground for ancient Africa and Europe. Though the Roman collapse ended the contacts that were developing between the African and European worlds, it did not spell utter catastrophe for them. Instead, the death of classical civilization actually facilitated their continued, if again isolated, development, for the barbarians absorbed and preserved many of the remnants of Roman civilization left in Europe while black Africa established and strengthened contacts with Rome's successors in northern Africa, the Moslems.

Sustained by their legacy from the Mediterranean world, medieval Europe and black Africa continued their development, almost oblivious of each other, for the next thousand years or so. Not until the opening of the Atlantic at the end of the fifteenth century did the two reestablish fruitful contacts. At that point black Africans became reluctant partners of the Europeans in the development and exploitation of the new-found American world.

Before going on to consider developments in Europe and Africa let us take a brief look at the lands and early peoples of the two worlds and note early contacts between the peoples of the Mediterranean and black Africa.

The Mediterranean Basin and Its People

Mediterranean peoples did not originate their civilization or in fact any appreciable part of it, but borrowed it, then transformed, adapted, and developed it. At every stage in its history, the Mediterranean Sea along with its coastland exercised a powerful, indeed determining if subtle, influence in shaping the adopted culture to meet its particular needs. Protected by narrow and relatively shallow outlets from the high tides and cold currents of the Atlantic, the Mediterranean lay placid, warm, and inviting. Moreover its coastal lands were narrow, separated from the hinterlands of the three continents by mountain ranges or, in the case of northeast Africa, deserts. Hence its peoples were encouraged, in fact forced, by geography to concentrate their attention on the sea itself. The climate of the whole basin, allowing for local variations, was uniform: hot, dry summers and rainy winters with marked seasonal changes. Because wetness and warmth, the two indispensables for natural and easy agriculture, did not occur at the same time, Mediterranean peoples had to resort to their own ingenuity to make up for the vagaries of nature.

Origins of Mediterranean Culture

The main borrowing place for Mediterranean civilization was southwestern Asia, just beyond the eastern end of the Mediterranean itself. Human-like creatures were roaming the earth 600,000 years ago, living in caves, experimenting with fire, shaping simple stone and bone tools, and eating fish, game, and one another. Gradually over the millennia they learned to live in groups, to follow herds of game wherever they went, and to construct shelters for themselves.

About 50,000 years ago man more or less as we know him today had emerged. He became a skilled hunter, improved his tools, developed the rudiments of social organization, began to bury his dead and make drawings and paintings on rocks and cave walls. But he was still dependent for his livelihood upon the bounty of nature. In the course of the five thousand years between 10,000 and 5,000 B.C., however, man learned to provide his own food by domesticating animals and planting crops. This development—usually spoken of as the Neolithic revolution, for man greatly improved his techniques of making stone tools and weapons in the process—opened the way to the founding of civilization. Southwestern Asia, an area that was much wetter and more fertile at that time than it is today, was where this revolution took place. By about the seventh millennium B.C. peoples living in the area that is now Iran, Turkey, and Jordan were grouped in permanent villages of twenty to two hundred houses, cultivating wheat, barley, peas, and lentils, and raising sheep, goats, cattle, pigs and dogs. They decorated their houses, fashioned a wide array of weapons and implements from stone, shell, raw copper and wood, produced basketry, textiles and pottery, and carried on trade for such items as obsidian, a granite-like volcanic rock prized for sharp-edged weapons. All in all, their life was comparable to, say, the ancient Pueblo culture of the American Southwest.

As the settled agricultural life produced a plentiful supply of food, population grew, increasing almost ten times in three thousand years. The increase in population led to expansion, and offshoots of the culture of the Iranian highlands appeared in the Tigris-Euphrates valley, where a Mesopotamian civilization flourished by the fourth millennium B.C. In addition to erecting a series of impressive city-states, these Sumerians of Mesopotamia, one of the earliest peoples to develop a civilization, perfected techniques for reducing copper, tin and lead from ores and for making bronze alloys. At the same time, they began to use boats extensively for river transport, and developed an extensive trade ranging from far inside Asia Minor to the Mediterranean.

The trade routes channeled into the Mediterranean both an abundance of goods and, more important in the long run, an enormous current of cultural influence. The current became even stronger in the third millennium when the independent cities of Mesopotamia were consolidated into a large and powerful empire stretching almost to the shores of the Mediterranean. Coastal cities at the eastern end of the Mediterranean, islands in the Aegean such as Cyprus and Crete, and the

Greek mainland itself began to be touched, and their life quickened, by ideas and commerce from the east. Influences also spread to Egypt where, under Asian tutelage, people learned to grow millet, cherries, and figs in the rich black soil of the Nile delta, to cultivate dates on the fringes of the Sahara desert, and to work copper. As in Asia, Egypt's cultural advance supported increases in population, expansion of trade, and extension of influence. The third-millennium penetration of the Mediterranean by Mesopotamia foreshadowed the blending of Asian, African and European elements into the formation of a series of Mediterranean empires.

The Mediterranean World and Black Africa

From about 1500 B.C. to about 500 A.D. the peoples living around the shores of the Mediterranean Sea participated in what has come to be called Mediterranean civilization. During its two thousand or so years of life, that civilization not only encompassed large areas of Asia, Africa, and Europe, but upon its demise left a legacy that was fundamental in shaping the histories of several areas that lay beyond its orbit, particularly northwestern Europe, sub-Saharan Africa, and the New World. Though the ancient Mediterranean world contained many different peoples and cultural traditions and was organized variously into city-states, principalities, kingdoms and empires, it might well be regarded as essentially a single civilization. As one major power after another sought with increasing success to dominate the entire Mediterranean basin, beliefs, values, ideas, styles, technologies, and institutions from the several cultures met and clashed, and by around 1500 B.C. merged to form composites. The succession of dominant powers provided the Mediterranean with a relatively continuous and stable political organization that facilitated trade and communication. The Egyptians were the first people to come to power in the Mediterranean, followed in succession by the Assyrians, Persians, and the Greeks. Minor or peripheral powers such as the Phoenicians, Hebrews and Carthaginians in the meantime also contributed significantly to the growing cultural and economic interchange. And finally the Romans, establishing their hegemony over the entire Mediterranean and its adjacent lands, completed the assimilation. In the early stages of its development, Mediterranean civilization maintained only tenuous ties with the barbarian communities of western Europe and with black Africa. During Greek and Roman times, however, knowledge of an interest in both of these neighboring areas grew, and commercial contacts with them increased greatly.

Egypt and Black Africa

From early times Egypt steadily pushed southward up the Nile, in the process absorbing influences from the interior of black Africa. Trade for Nubian gold from the hills between the Nile and the Red Sea was carried on well before the unification of Egypt, and afterwards regular contacts developed with the upper reaches of the Nile, the African Sudan country, and what is modern Ethiopia and Somalia. In 2275 B.C. a pharaoh sent four expeditions to the south that returned with three hundred asses carrying incense, ebony, ivory, leopard and panther skins, throwing sticks, and a Pygmy. Although by the 1880's B.C. the pharoahs were forced to fortify their southern borders against raiders from the black Nubian kingship upriver, they still encouraged commercial intercourse. But when the Egyptian Middle Kingdom fell on hard days, the Nubians successfully renewed their attacks and, in the confusion surrounding the collapse of the Middle Kingdom, won temporary domination of Egypt and a black pharaoh ruled.

But with the establishment of the New Kingdom, Egypt recovered her equilibrium, turned the tables on her old adversary, and conquered and incorporated the whole Nubian kingdom into her empire. Shortly afterwards the famous Egyptian queen Hatshepsut, sent out five ships on a voyage to the land of Punt, probably in the vicinity of Modern Somalia. The expedition returned with a fabulous cargo including ostrich feathers and eggs, cinnamon wood, tropical plants for the royal gardens, a live panther, some cattle, immense amounts of gold, and numerous slaves. Egyptian tombs and temples contained many paintings depicting black Africans. Often they were shown transporting the wealth of trade goods that Egypt got from the interior, including articles such as bowls, baskets, jars, weapons, shields, and miniature models of interior towns and cities.

Because of striking similarities between Egyptian and black African kingship—we shall examine the latter in a subsequent chapter—some authorities believe that the very character of the Egyptian monarchy was the result of early influences from the interior. Like many black African rulers, Egypt's pharoahs were thought of as living gods, incorporating in their persons, during their tenure as rulers, the powers of deity. They were believed to be the reincarnation of the god Horus, the "Great God" or "Lord of Heaven," and their special charge was the maintenance of harmonious relations between human society and the forces of nature. Thus the kings were an indispensable link or bond between man and the world in which he lived. As such they were accorded special treatment befitting their special status. A pharaoh's name was never pronounced. He was addressed only indirectly by one of his many titles or spoken of simply as "one." He was surrounded, and largely isolated, by an elaborate official and religious ceremonial, and his person was kept groomed to cosmetic perfection by an elaborate ritualistic toilet. Often pharaohs married their own "Queen Sisters" as the god Horus was said to have done, thereby conserving and fortifying the divine blood. As divine kings, Egyptian rulers were able to impose upon their people a degree of autocratic government unknown elsewhere in the ancient world. Moreover, they left some elements of a conception of divine kingship as a legacy to the western world, remnants of which lingered in Europe until the twentieth century A.D.

Following the collapse of Egypt, the Hebrews and Phoenicians developed an extensive trade with the interior of Africa and were soon taking home such luxuries and curiosities as ivory, apes, and peacocks and, most important of all, gold. By 800 B.C. the Phoenicians had established commercial bases on the coasts of North Africa and beyond the Gibraltar strait as far away perhaps as the coast of northwest Africa. The city of Carthage, originally a Phoenician anchorage on the Gulf of Tunis, broke away from her Phoenician mother and established herself as an independent city-state. By 500 B.C. Carthaginian fleets dominated western Mediterranean waters and had explored some of the Atlantic coast of Africa. A certain Hanno was reported to have sailed down the west coast of Africa to an island called "Cerne" where the Carthaginians traded perfume, wine, and pottery to black Africans for lion and leopard skins and elephant hides and tusks. The Africans were described as using ivory for drinking cups and bracelets and household ornaments. The Carthaginians also established trans-Saharan trade with black Africans and were soon the chief purveyors of African gold, ivory, wild animals and slaves to the Mediterranean world.

Greek Civilization

Though we know little about the peoples who inhabited the early Mycenaean or Greek cities, the design and workmanship of the weapons, chariots, pottery, masks, and the types of whetstones and gems they used provide clear evidence that they were in contact not only with the islands of the Mediterranean, but with the hinterlands of Europe and Africa as well. Eventually the Greeks established colonies in southern and western Italy, on Sicily, in southern France, and in Egypt. Their settlers in Egypt sent back home news of black peoples to the south and southwest of Egypt whom they called collectively "Ethiopians." By the sixth century B.C. Greeks had located the homeland of the "Ethiopians" who had been mentioned in Greek literature as early as the time of Homer in sub-Saharan Africa, and were familiar with many of the individual black cultures. Herodotus, the most famous Greek geographer and historian, himself traveled up the Nile and supplemented his personal observations with interviews with people living in the locality in order to leave a description of the black civilizations of the area. We have mention of several other Greek writers making similar trips. Though the full texts of their observations have not come down to us, fragments indicate that the Greeks were fascinated by black African skills in archery and elephant hunting, as well as their customs of plural marriages and nudity.

When Alexander the Great (336-323 B.C.), conquered Egypt, he founded the city of Alexandria on the coast and made it a great melting pot for Greeks, Asians and Africans. By 200 B.C. it was the greatest city of the known world, a dazzling metropolis famous for its commerce, wealth, culture, and science. From the interior of Africa, Alexandria's merchants procured gold, ivory, fine woods, scented oils, cotton, wild animals (always one of Africa's chief exports during ancient as well as modern times) and some slaves for re-sale in other Mediterranean ports. Recent excavations of Greek colonial sites in southern Italy have furnished evidence of the destination of at least some of the black slaves sent from Africa: one wall painting shows a white man boxing with a Negro, presumably a slave gladiator.

Though very few blacks lived in the ancient Greek world, writers from the time of Homer on occasion referred to them and artists depicted them. It is clear that the Negro in both literature and art was most often a conventional symbol or type, but there are examples that seem to be portraits of individuals as well. Ethiopians generally symbolized the virtues of justice and piety, and, accordingly, mythological heroes who manifested these qualities were frequently depicted as black-skinned. For example, Memnon, who went to aid Priam at Troy, was said to be the black king of Ethiopia. Similarly, Greek artists sometimes used Negro faces and figures purely as stylistic devices, but just as surely sometimes betrayed a genuine interest in portraying their curious subjects.

The Roman Empire and Black Africa

By 31 B.C. Rome had wrested control of the western Mediterranean and much of North Africa from Carthage, conquered Greece, the remnants of the realm of Alexander, and Egypt. The entire Mediterranean was unified for the first time in its history and for almost the next five hundred years constituted the Roman world. Though the Romans never incorporated much of Africa beyond the Sahara desert into their empire, they were well aware of its existence. Many travelers', and mariners' stories circulated during Roman times about remote and mysterious black Africa, and the Romans made some attempts at exploration. In the second century B.C., Polybius reported sailing beyond the Strait of Gibraltar, and a century later Roman explorers reached the Canaries and other islands off the Atlantic coast of what is now southern Morocco. Recent excavations on that and other nearby sites indicate occupation of the area by Mediterranean people from as early as the seventh century B.C. After Augustus annexed Egypt he became interested in the peoples beyond its frontiers and sent expeditions up the Nile into Nubia where they established outposts and trading stations. The Romans also made expeditions across the Sahara from at least the first century B.C. onward, pushing as far as the big-game country of the savanna. The emperor Septimius Severus, himself a native of what is now Libya, was particularly interested in the African hinterland and the trans-Saharan trade, and had posts and settlements established far into the desert. He also enlisted many black African troops in his armies, some of whom were stationed in Europe. Modern archaeological investigation has unearthed Roman lamps, pottery, engraved glass, beads, and coins in the southern Sahara region, indicating considerable trade through the area.

Though there is no way to judge the number of blacks resident in the Roman empire, they were there in sufficient numbers for Roman writers to make frequent references to them in their works and for Roman artists to portray them almost as a matter of course. Some blacks were brought in as captives or slaves, but others, apparently free, made names for themselves as famous boxers, acrobats, jockies, and athletes. One writer tells of 100 Negro huntsmen presented in a circus in 61 B.C., and comments that on one occasion the entire audience at the theater was black. The famous writer Martial saw enough "kinky haired Ethiopians" at the opening of the Colosseum to remark upon their number, and other Roman satirists often made jokes about mixed liaisons and unexpected mulatto babies. The Latin language developed an extensive and complex vocabulary for describing varying degrees of blackness and the many shades of copper-toned skin prevalent in Rome.

The Roman empire slipped into decline toward the end of the second century A.D. and, by the end of the sixth century, had almost completely disintegrated. Instead of one world, the Mediterranean at that point became three worlds. In Greece and Asia Minor the imperial tradition continued, though much orientalized, as the Eastern or Byzantine Empire. The Levantine, Egyptian, and North African portions of the old empire fell to the forces of Islam after 600 and became important parts of a new Moslem civilization. And Christian Mediterranean and western Europe, already weak and divided, drifted into the economic stagnation and cultural blight that characterized the early centuries of the European Middle Ages.

Beyond each of the three divisions into which the old empire had fallen lay areas of the world that had never been a part of Roman civilization—the interior of Asia, barbarian Europe, and Africa below the Sahara. We shall take little notice, from here on, of the eastern Mediterranean and its adjacent Asian lands, for that area has little relevance to our story. But we must pay close attention to Africa and the more westerly part of Europe because their histories, though differing greatly in detail, developed along generally parallel lines.

African Lands and Peoples

South of the narrow fertile strip along the coast of northern Africa that was a part of the Mediterranean world, a desert area larger than the United States—the Sahara—formed an effective natural frontier. Beyond that arid barrier was the black African world. Black Africa, today accounted an underdeveloped area, was, in the early stages of human history, not only the most developed continent but possibly the place where man himself originated.

Africa south of the Sahara is a vast and sprawling area of over six and a half million square miles—more than half again the size of Europe and twice that of the United States. The larger part of it, some eighty percent, is savanna, grassland like the American prairie, where the climate is roughly comparable to that of the southern United States. The other twenty percent of sub-Saharan Africa is tropical rain forest, or jungle, characterized by extremely heavy rainfall—averaging around seventy inches per year, comparable to the deep south of the United States, but reaching four hundred inches a year in some places. A few isolated highlands strung north-south through east-central Africa have temperate climates.

Today's rocky and sandy Sahara was, in the remote past, both less extensive and less arid, and consequently the peoples of the continent found it easier both to travel across and to live in. Gradually, however, it began to dry up and expand, leaving only a few isolated fertile oases. The desiccation forced the Saharan peoples to move to more hospitable areas to the north and the south. Those who moved south were limited to maintaining only a few hazardous routes of passage across the desert to the Mediterranean World.

Immediately south of the Sahara lies the four-hundred-mile-wide Sudan belt of savanna, stretching from the Atlantic on the west to the highlands of Ethiopia in the east, and winding its way down through the center of the continent to South Africa where it broadens into a veld. The sudan belt and the veld are steppe, open land covered with grasses of five to twenty feet in height and only widely separated clumps of deciduous trees. Summers are rainy, hot, and humid, and winters are dry, windy, and dusty. Such grasslands are excellent grazing grounds, and antelopes, zebras, giraffes, elephants and buffaloes, as well as domesticated cattle, flourish there, along with their predators, lions, leopards, hyenas, flies and mosquitoes.

Astride the equator, and stretching from the center of Africa to the Atlantic and up along the north coast of the Gulf of Guinea, is the tropical rain forest. This jungle area is characterized by monotonous heat hovering around eighty degrees Fahrenheit, with little daily or seasonal change, and high humidity produced by the unusually heavy rainfall. In this hothouse climate luxuriantly thick and tangled vegetation flourishes, obscuring streams and ponds with its wavy green canopy and blocking the sunlight almost completely from the barren gloom underneath. Mahogany, ebony, walnut and rubber trees grow beside the mangrove. Most big game is absent, but birds, fish, snakes, monkeys and apes multiply along with crocodiles, hippopotamuses and tsetses.

Desert, steppe, jungle, and mountain, Africa's natural terrain has always proved harsh and difficult to manage. Even her rivers are un- suited to extensive human use. Rising in rainy interior uplands they descend by stages to the sea, broken frequently and abruptly by falls and rapids that limit navigation to short distances. Even in the lower courses of most, navigation is limited to shallow and shifting channels through extensive deltas. Equally limited in use are Africa's productive soils. Her best soils are those found on alluvial river plains such as that of the Nile, in volcanic areas in parts of the East African highlands, and in some of the grasslands in the high veld of South Africa. But even these are not comparable to European or American soils, for they are less durable and tend to lose their fertility quickly under cultivation, as do the reddish tropical soils once they are cleared of their lush natural vegetation.

Homo Sapiens Origin

In spite of the inhospitable environment—or perhaps because of it— Africa seems probably to have been the place of origin of the human species. Increasingly, archaeological discoveries suggest that man, distin- guished from other highly developed primates by his use of tools to supplement his hands, feet and teeth, originated in the region around Lake Victoria, whence he spread through the rest of Africa and into Asia and Europe. It is possible to distinguish four basic groups of early men in Africa, though the questions of their relationships to each other (*e.g.*, did they develop from a common ancestor type, or originate independently, or result from admixtures) are still the subject of much debate among scholars. The small yellowish-brown *bushmen* types seem to have spread generally southward into south-central and east Africa and northward towards Ethiopia and the Sahara. Four to five feet tall, light brown *Pygmies* moved westward into the central Congo and on to the rain forests of West Africa, and along with the bushmen were dis- tinct well before 100,000 B.C. A *Caucasian type*, sometimes called Chushits or Hamites, somewhat later spread along the Mediterranean and Atlantic coasts of North Africa, along the Afro-Asian coasts of the Red Sea, and seem eventually to have spilled over into Asia and Europe.

Finally, sometime around 6,000 B.C., a distinct dark brown or black *Negroid* type, whose exact origins still present the most questions, emerged and settled in the Sahara and the Sudan belt of savanna country stretching from West Africa to the upper Nile valley. They were perhaps the largest group.

The question of language development among the peoples of Africa is difficult because the picture is complicated, even more than it is most places in the world, by linguistic borrowings, buffeting, adaptations, and fusions. Of all man's cultural accoutrements, language is the one that he changes most readily and easily. But a few general patterns can be discerned. The African Caucasians' descendants spoke Semitic languages in Arabia and the Near East, Berber in North Africa, Cushitic in Ethiopia, and Ancient Egyptian along the Nile. The bushman group developed Khoisan languages—with the distinctive "click" sounds—still spoken in many of their areas of Africa, while the pygmies seem to have either developed little in the way of an original language or to have dropped it early in favor of adopting the languages of the various peoples with whom they came in contact, particularly those who conquered or dominated them. The Negroes developed a large group of languages called Nigritic or Niger-Congo with many modern subdivisions and branches such as Mande, Ibo, Yoruba, and Bantu.

The Sahara and the African Sudan, the areas inhabited by Negroid peoples, did not undergo the spectacular climatic changes associated with the Ice Ages that left their mark so clearly on ancient Europe. Consequently, dating artifacts surviving from cultures of Africa's remote past is rendered extremely difficult. Moreover, relatively little faunal evidence of the sort that we have for Europe—skeletal remains—has been uncovered in Africa because that continent's acid soils quickly destroy organic materials, even bones, almost as soon as they are deposited. Thus, though a wealth of stone tools and weapons from early African cultures are being turned up by archaeologists, we have only scant knowledge, as yet, of the men who made and used them.

We have evidence of human cultures in various parts of Africa from as early as 1,000,000 years ago, the time when the Ice Ages were just beginning in Europe. But the first West African culture of which we can form a general picture is the Sangoan dating from around 100,000 B.C. The Sangoan was a woodland and waterside rather than a hunting culture. Sangoan peoples trapped small animals, did rough woodworking,

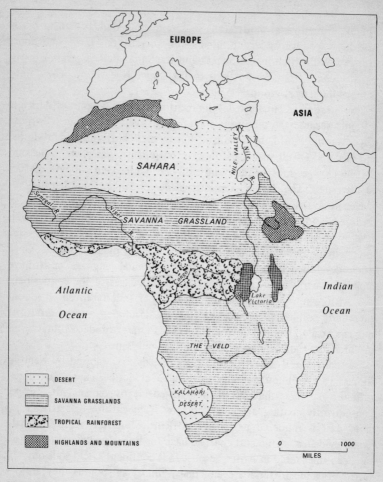

Main Features of African Geography

navigated rivers with rudimentary rafts or canoes, knew the use of fire, and used digging picks, probably to unearth wild yams and perhaps to cultivate them.

Although a kind of proto-agriculture based on the cultivation of tubers such as the yam might well have been practiced far back into the

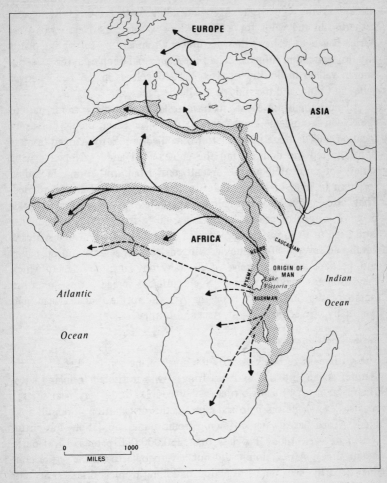

Probable Spread of Man in Africa. Shaded areas represent heaviest population density at the time of the discovery of America.

Paleolithic period, true agriculture—involving the preparation of the ground for actual planting of the crop as well as the cultivation of it—evolved in Africa, as it did on other parts of the world, only much later. West Africa was in fact one of the four spots on the globe where agriculture originated. Until around 6,000 B.C. the entire world remained in the Old Stone Age, depending upon hunting, fishing and gathering in the wilds for a living. Shortly after, the Negroes of West Africa began to reshape their natural environment by cultivating plants and domesticating animals, as had the Caucasoid peoples in the Mesopotamian valleys in Southwest Asia, the Mongoloids in the Yellow River valley in China, and the Indians in Middle America.

African agriculture seems to have originated in the extreme part of the Sudan around the headwaters of the Niger River, though the exact location and date are still a matter of conjecture. Early African farmers domesticated the donkey and the guinea fowl and developed a wide variety of cultivated plants, or cultigens, from wild forms, including sorghum (a kind of corn), millet (a cereal staple), and a form of rice. They also cultivated watermelons, squash-like gourds, several varieties of yams, a type of peanut, okra, tamarind (a fruit tree), and kola nuts (still used in flavoring modern "cola" drinks). In addition, the Africans developed several oil producing cultigens such as sesame and oil palms and, perhaps most impressive of all, a cotton plant, the fibers of which they used for making textiles. Such cultigens spread across the entire length of the Sudan belt, from the Atlantic to the Indian Ocean, and eventually into ancient Egypt, Asia and Europe.

Earliest Settlements

The settlement of black Africa—the areas of the continent south of the Mediterranean and the Red Sea fringes—was restricted to inland sites. There was no significant settlement of peoples on or very near the sea coasts. Several factors help account for this distribution of population. First, Africa has always suffered chronic underpopulation—the entire continent even today has less than 250,000,000 people. Until quite recent times, Africa simply did not have people to fill the entire continent, partly because of disabling or killing tropical diseases. Second was the lack of foodstuffs—not one of the world's major food crops was native to Africa. She had to import all of them and adapt them to her soils and climate, and she acquired all relatively late in her history. Third, and perhaps most important from the historian's viewpoint, was the fact that most of black Africa, lacking the advantages of a large population as well as natural harbors and easily navigable rivers, was for the entirety of its early history oriented towards the Sahara Desert. Black African's main contacts with the outside world were through

Saharan trade routes rather than via the wider prospects of their own coasts. The inland orientation of the continent remained unchanged until the Atlantic Ocean was opened at Africa's back door at the end of the fifteenth century.

Ancient Europe

Unlike the huge rounded land mass that is Africa, Europe is small in area (4,000,000 square miles), has irregular coasts full of natural harbors, and possesses many easily navigable rivers. Europe is a long narrow peninsula of Asia, deeply serrated by inland seas and bays that pinch the continent at many places into relatively narrow isthmuses. As a result, there is no place in central or western Europe that is more than 350 miles from a seacoast. Only in what is now mid-Soviet Russia does any land lie more than 500 miles from the sea, and even the inland areas of most of Europe are connected to the sea by vast river systems. Beyond the Mediterranean lands, where the rivers are narrow, swift, and shallow, Europe's rivers are generally wide, deep, and sluggish, ideally suited to navigation. Unlike the rivers on most other continents, they are generally free of rapids and waterfalls. Moreover, the lower courses of many of them form deep natural estuaries that are capable of admitting ocean vessels for considerable distances. And they span the continent, in many places virtually linking the coasts.

Europe's proximity to the ocean and seas has also brought it the favors of good climate. Although located in northerly latitudes—most of it lies well to the north of Chicago or New York City—Europe enjoys relatively mild temperatures and ample precipitation for sustaining agriculture. Warm currents, originating in the tropical parts of the Atlantic, flow northward and eastward to wash the shores of Europe during the winter months, and winds blowing across these waters carry warmth to much of the continent. The same westerly winds bring the plentiful rainfall. Europe is also favored above Africa, and most other continents, in having almost no uninhabitable deserts, Arctic wastes, or plateaus too high to allow normal human activities. And it is entirely free from the burdens imposed by tropical heat and rain forests.

If Europe is strikingly different from Africa in these general geographic respects, it is, in its relation to the Mediterranean basin, somewhat similar to Africa. As the greater part of Africa was effectively

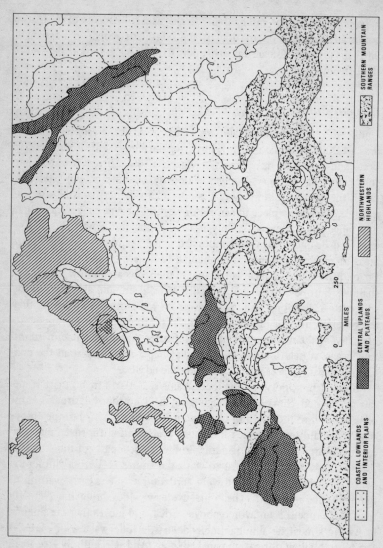

Main Features of Europe: Geography

separated from Mediterranean civilization through much of its early history by the Sahara desert, most of Europe was separated but not sealed off from the Mediterranean by another sort of natural barricade. A great highland barrier stretches across southern Europe, a short distance inland, from the Cantabrian mountains on the west coast of Spain, through the Pyrenees, the Massif Central in southern France, the great Alps in north Italy, Switzerland, and Austria, the Yugoslav highlands, and the Pindus range in Greece, to the Balkan mountains near the Black Sea. Occasional breaks in this long mountain chain provide passes through which populations, commerce, and culture flowed from the Mediterranean basin into the European hinterland. Once beyond the mountains, early peoples could move down river valleys and across the great European plain with relative ease.

Mankind's Development in Europe

Human history began considerably later in Europe than in Africa. Only towards the end of the Ice Ages that from *ca.* 1,000,000 B.C. to *ca.* 25,000 B.C. covered much of Europe with great glaciers did *homo sapiens* appear in western Europe. Coming from southwestern Asia or northeastern Africa, where Australoid and proto-Negroid *homo sapiens*, forerunners of modern man, were already well established, these nomadic food gatherers, fishermen, and hunters possessed various stone tools and hunting weapons, and were skilled in making clothing of skins and furs. Gradually they settled among the older more primitive *homo erectus* living in Europe. The mode of life of the newcomers did not change substantially for the next 25,000 to 30,000 years. Many lived in caves, the walls of which they sometimes painted with their now famous and familiar hunting scenes. Others constructed hut-like shelters for themselves by digging out large holes in the ground and roofing them with boughs, stones and dirt. They also made tent-like structures by stretching skins over rows of large mammoth bones and tusks stuck into the ground to form posts.

Dependent upon the supplies of mammoths, wild horses, bison and particularly reindeer, these peoples moved frequently, following the herds. They could not have settled down and developed agriculture, even had they been so disposed, because Europe, during the millenia of the Ice Ages had, instead of the lush vegetation that exists there today, only sparse and stunted stubble growth. But herds of wild animals were plentiful, and the geography of Pleistocene Europe favored nomadic movement. Not yet given its familiar modern-day outlines by the inundation that occurred as the last glaciers melted, Europe was still almost a solid land mass relatively uninterrupted by mountains, lakes or seas. Britain, for example, was not an island but a peninsula of Europe, for the English Channel had not yet been formed. Today's Thames River in England was then still a branch of the Rhine that flowed through lowlands that later sank to form part of the bottom of the modern North Sea. Even the Mediterranean was, at times during the Pleistocene or Ice Ages, only a series of lakes with land bridges connecting Europe with Africa. Thus the early Europeans not only followed their herds from England to Siberia, but, in earlier periods, managed intercourse with Africa as well.

The retreat of the ice around 8,000 B.C. and the consequent warming of the area changed Europe's vegetation, as well as its geography, and facilitated cultural advances. Water from the melting glaciers settled in the lowland to form today's seas and channels, while land masses that had been suppressed by the weight of the continental glaciers rose again to form the highlands of modern northern and central Europe. In the new damp and warm climate, stunted sub-arctic flora gave way to grasslands and woodlands, and the reindeer to the red deer and the elk and the wild ox. Humans found their condition much improved. Food gathering in the forests and swamps, and fishing in the warm waters, was generally much easier, while the difficulties of tracking the smaller, less gregarious game of the woods were lessened by the domestication of the dog. But life, though greatly eased compared to that of the Ice Ages, remained nomadic and uncertain, dependent upon the fortunes of food gathering. This stage of development remained characteristic of the whole of Europe for the next three thousand years, and continued in isolated spots for another two thousand years after that. During the latter period, however, most of Europe's population began taking the final great step—the cultivation of food.

Development of Systematic Agriculture

The introduction of agriculture, of the Neolithic Revolution as it is often called, came late to western Europe. From southwestern Asia, where the agricultural revolution had taken shape around 6,000 B.C., semi-nomadic groups, carrying with them the new knowledge of food production, began to wander up the Danube valley and move westward across the calm Aegean and Mediterranean Seas. They settled in agricultural villages, and generation after generation advanced gradually farther westward. As these groups moved into a new area they burned off the woodlands and began to till the soil between the charred stumps with their stone hoes and digging sticks. Generally they avoided the open plains because the thick grass cover there proved too tough for their primitive tools to subdue. By perhaps 5000 B.C. the Danube valley had been brought under cultivation, though communities of hunting cultures continued to exist there side by side with the new farming communities as they would all over Europe for many centuries to come. In another thousand years central Europe, the Rhine valley, and the Iberian peninsula were colonized; in another thousand France and Italy; and finally, by around 2500 B.C. England and Scandinavia had entered the agricultural age.

Trade and Crafts

During the same centuries that agriculture was coming into Europe, knowledge of metalworking likewise seeped in from the Near East. The new age of metals was not just a time when European peoples began to make their hard-edged tools and weapons of bronze. More importantly, the use of metals brought about new long-distance trade, not only in copper and tin, necessary for making bronze, but rarer luxury commodities such as gold and amber. Increased trade, in turn, made possible the exchange and propagation of new ideas that were never possible under former circumstances. By shortly after 2000 B.C. south-central European peoples were in contact with metalwork merchants in faraway Syria, and Mycenaean objects, motifs and techniques were appearing regularly in the barbarian cultures. In a few centuries an elaborate network of trade routes for the exchange of amber and tin linked England, Jutland, and the Baltic with the head of the Adriatic by way of trade routes across central Europe.

The barbarian European world reached its culmination with the Celts. Identified as early as the second millenium B.C., Celtic culture matured about 500 B.C. and lasted in full bloom until it disintegrated under pressures from the Germans and the Romans. Our knowledge of their world comes from a large store of archaeological evidence, comments by Greek and Roman writers, and actual Celtic vernacular tradition that survived among Celts living in isolation in Ireland long enough to be written down in the Middle Ages. The examples of Celtic art and craftsmanship that archaeologists have recovered are among the most impressive from anywhere in the ancient world. The numerous pieces of gold and silver jewelry, the bronze and iron weapons, armor, cups, flagons, fire dogs, cauldrons, hand-mirrors, as well as the stores of decorated pots produced by the Celts are spectacular, and the remains of their houses, tombs, carts, chariots, and wagons are imposing. Classical writers paid tribute to the Celts for their fighting ability, their hard drinking habits, their horsemanship, and their love of equestrian sports and exercises that were the forerunners of Medieval jousts and tournaments. The Celts' own folk literature mirrored a tribal, hierarchical society ruled by a king and comprised of two privileged classes in addition to the body of the ordinary people. One of the privileged groups was a warrior aristocracy, and the other was made up of the "men of art"—priests, poets, artists, and craftsmen. It was through the work of the latter group that a large part of the Celtic heritage was handed down to Medieval and Modern Europe and western civilization.

The African and European cultures that had existed alongside ancient Mediterranean civilization, one to the north and the other to the south, would continue to develop, each in virtual isolation, for another five hundred years or so after the demise of Mediterranean civilization. In the chapters that follow we shall sketch the outlines of their histories and compare some of the institutions and problems that distinguished each and brought the two together in the New World after 1492.

CHAPTER TWO

Religion and Politics in Europe and Africa

Europe and Africa were for much of their early histories split between two cultures. Ancient Mediterranean civilization encompassed roughly the northern third of Africa and the southern third of Europe. Beyond these Mediterranean areas, the other two-thirds of both continents remained in virtual isolation. Isolation, however, did not mean that these areas were devoid of either people or civilization. Both black Africa and barbarian Europe produced independent cultures parallel to, if less refined than, those of the Mediterranean basin. The picture was thus composed of three parts. At the center lay the brilliant Mediterranean culture that lasted from about 1500 B.C. to about 500 A.D., while to the south Africa developed its own indigenous civilization, and to the north Europe did the same. Mediterranean culture reached full flower under Roman auspices, only to wither when the empire met with troubled times. Following the collapse of Rome, Moslem conquerors fell heirs to the Egyptian and North African segments of the old empire, and Moslem merchants and missionaries gradually established contacts with black Africa, hitherto almost completely isolated. Similarly, after the collapse of centralized Roman government, the third or so of Europe that had been part of the Roman Empire fell under the control of various local conquerors, some of them former Roman generals or governors, others Germanic chieftains. In the following several centuries, those areas of Europe retaining a hold on the remnants of classical civilization gradually established contact with the "barbaric," *i.e.*, non-romanized, peoples who inhabited the western and northern European hinterlands.

The Christian-Roman Imprint on Europe

The meeting of Mediterranean culture with the indigenous culture of Europe's hinterland resulted in blendings. Western and northern European culture did not develop uniformly. Southwestern Europe, including what is now Italy, Spain and much of France, was thoroughly Romanized, and consequently its civilization relatively homogeneous. Beyond that area, however, to the north, the east, and the extreme west, lay regions that had enjoyed little or no Roman influence. In the northern and western British Isles, northern France, and Germany native barbarian cultures had emerged.

Influence of the Missionaries

But if the Roman Empire was dead, the zeal for expansion was not. The new goal was not conquest of territory, but souls. Instead of soldiers the Romanized areas now sent out Christian missionaries. Between about the years 500 and 1000, missionaries flooded into northern Europe gradually converting the barbarians and, in the process, transmitting to them at least an awareness of some of the classical world's values and institutions.

The role of the Christian missionaries in northern and, later, eastern Europe was not dissimilar to that of the Moslem conquerors and merchants who were responsible for making the first significant contacts with sub-Saharan Africa. The conversion of Europe was a slow process, not complete until about the time Columbus discovered America. One of the lasting effects of the work of the missionaries was the development of a priestly class in Medieval Europe—a praying class that complemented the knightly fighting class and the servile working class. In each region of Europe, Christian, Roman and barbarian traditions slowly but surely blended. The result was a series of regional variations in culture that still characterize the continent. Both Africa and Europe thus inherited substantial legacies from their own pasts to which they both added rich ingredients inherited from the Mediterranean world. Both the civilization that took shape in Africa and the one that emerged in Europe under the impact of post-Roman Mediterranean influences were new products. The new African culture flourished in several black Islamic states that dominated that continent between the eighth and the end of the fifteenth centuries, while the new European culture assumed the features of the more familiar Medieval civilization that characterized western and central Europe during the same period.

The Influence of Roman Settlements

Even before the work of the Christian missionaries began, the Romans had put their stamp on Europe's future by establishing a pattern of settlement that prevailed for centuries. The typical Roman settlement consisted of a villa that eventually developed into a community. Roman colonization of Europe through the establishing of villas was determined almost entirely by the proximity of towns, roads and frontiers to usable land. Roman towns functioned as market places for the surrounding countryside and hence became the nuclei of economic growth in the Roman world of subsistence economics. As such, they were a natural place around which to establish more villas. The Roman frontier with its military camps and forts was, like the town, a major market area for agricultural produce. Moreover, the frontier supplied manpower for agricultural development—veteran soldiers, families of officers, officials, and merchants and, not infrequently, immigrants from beyond the frontier. And Roman roads, connecting the towns and fortresses, lent security, for they provided protection to Romans and served as symbols of law and order to the less civilized neighbors. Romans adjacent to the hinterlands of Europe tended to settle and bring under cultivation lands of a type with which they were already familiar in Italy—light soils, easily cultivable loams, silt and semi-arid

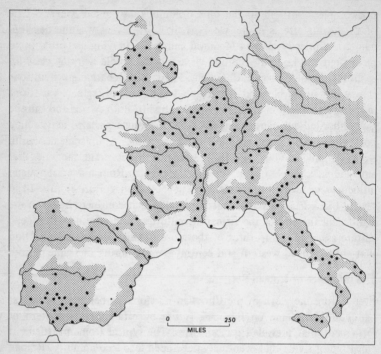

Settlement Patterns of Roman Empire. Dots represent important towns and shaded areas heaviest population density.

areas—at least when such soils could be found along their roads and frontiers and around their towns. Generally speaking, they kept away from hard clays and damp forests. The result was a Roman pattern of settlement that concentrated population in western Europe along the inland routes rather than along the sea coasts, a pattern similar to that of Africa's early settlement. The striking exception to this pattern was on the Iberian peninsula where the coastal periphery provided the requisite markets, protection, and soils—a factor, perhaps, to be taken into consideration when accounting for Spain and Portugal being the first European nations to venture successfully into the Atlantic Ocean many centuries later.

First Waves of Immigrations

The movement of peoples about Europe during the early centuries of the Medieval period created new ethnic and linguistic divisions in some-what the same way that the great migrations in Africa determined its modern makeup. Even so, more often than not the general patterns of settlement already established by the Romans in Europe were con-tinued. The European migrations occurred in three major waves: the Germanic migrations that began in the latter days of the Roman Em-pire, the invasions of Scandinavians and Arabs from the eighth to the tenth centuries, and the expansion into eastern Europe in the late twelfth and thirteenth centuries. In most cases populations involved in these migrations were quite small by modern standards. Europe was still so sparsely populated during these centuries that the movement of no more than a few thousand people could permanently alter linguistic and ethnic lines. But by the end of the thirteenth century, Europe's num-bers had grown to such proportions that such modifications could no longer be easily brought about.

Migrations in Africa

The peopling of Africa by its modern inhabitants was, like the peopling of Europe, a long and complex process involving migrations of groups about the continent from prehistoric times on. While in Europe the modern pattern of settlement was more or less fixed by the series of Germanic, Arabic, Scandinavian and Slavic migrations that took place between the latter days of the Roman Empire and the end of the Middle Ages, in Africa the process continued until the eighteenth cen-tury. Of the countless migrations, the one that produced the single greatest alteration in the human geography of black Africa was that of the Bantu. The predominately Negroid Bantu-speaking people living in the Cameroon Highlands experienced a population explosion about the time of Christ and began to move to less thickly settled areas of the continent. They penetrated the Congo basin to the south and, by around 1000 A.D., had discovered and settled the open and fertile lake country of east Africa. Gradually during the next eight hundred years or so they spread northward and southward to gradually populate the present-day Bantu areas of Africa.

Christian and Islamic Influences in Africa

Mediterranean Africa, belonging to the Roman world, was thoroughly Christianized by the fourth century. Indeed, it produced several of the architects of the early Christian church—to name a few, Saints Tertullian, Cyprian, and Cyril, Origan, Athanasius, and, the most famous of all, St. Augustine of Hippo. In the Nile valley, Christianity replaced the old Egyptian gods, and in North Africa it replaced the primitive religions of the Berbers. In the upper Nile, for example, Christians, after converting the kingdom of Meroe, renamed it Nubia and pushed on to win dominance in Axum, the predecessor state of Ethiopia. The new religion, in its various Latin, Orthodox and heretical forms, pushed steadily southward during the next three centuries, converting much of Africa north of the rain forests except the Niger valley and the very headwaters of the Nile. Some die-hard pagans from Carthage seem to have moved out of reach of the Christian wave, preserving their older religions and carrying them into black Africa, particularly into the area of the ancient empire of Ghana.

Africa south of the Sahara developed its own forms of religion. These early religions sought to enable men to find ways of behaving towards the realities they apprehended immediately around them—natural forces, the felt influence of parents and grandparents even after they were dead, and the powers sensed within individuals and in social institutions. This quest produced a variegated pattern of nature worship, ancestor veneration, and concern about components of the individual psyche such as courage, cowardice and loyalty. As men became aware of themselves and their immediate environment in relationship to a larger setting, they developed more complex conceptions of god-like figures and wove about them a mythology. Doubtless over the centuries some foreign ideas and forms were added to these indigenous religions, particularly elements from the old cults of the north coast brought by the pagans pushed south by the spread of Christianity.

A third religious force entered Africa during the seventh century in the form of Islam, spread by marauding armies from Arabia. In 639 Moslem armies entered Egypt; five years later they swept as far west as Carthage; and within a century had conquered the rest of North Africa and were invading Spain. Only Ethiopia, isolated in its highlands, was able to withstand the onslaught and remain Christian. For some generations Mediterranean Africa prospered under her new masters and the influence of her new religion, as the Moslems assimilated the best of the old Mediterranean culture and infused it with new life. After the eleventh century, however, though some areas such as Egypt continued to prosper, much of the central North African coastal region—the Maghrib—fell into troubled times as a new wave of invaders arrived from Arabia via Egypt. Dynastic quarrels, internecine struggles, misgovernment and local wars fostered by the new invasions disrupted the civilization of this area long so important to black Africa because of its trade across the Sahara. As forests were denuded and agricultural lands devastated, the desert crept in, the economy faltered, and the trans-Saharan trade routes shifted farther to the west. They were then exploited more and more by Moslem Berbers who had established themselves along the Atlantic coast of Africa as far as Senegal.

Islam's Spread South of the Sahara

Though the waves of Moslem territorial and political conquest did not cross the desert southward, the religion and culture that the Arabs brought with them did, carried by merchants. The whole savanna belt south of the Sahara gradually became Islamic as one after another of the black empires converted and adopted much of Moslem culture. Islam became the religion and Arabic the language of most of the ruling, commercial and educated classes, reflecting the wealth and prestige that these groups represented. Even the name of the savanna strip—Sudan—was an Arabic word meaning the "black people." For the next several centuries much of black Africa was economically, culturally, and politically oriented to the Moslem-dominated Mediterranean world.

Learning was from the beginning the brilliant and unifying thread running through the whole tapestry of Islam. Central to Islamic learning was the Koran, the collected revelations made to the founder of the faith, Mohammed the Prophet. All Moslem learning, law, and science was focused on this work. The Islamic faith thus was the basis of Moslem scholarship as well as a political and legal unifying force. Black African empires as they adopted the learning embraced the faith. Great black African imperial capitals such as Timbuktu and Djenne rivaled the most important North African cities as centers of Moslem learning, particularly from the fifteenth to the seventeenth centuries. Schools of Moorish and Berber scholars in Timbuktu and eminent black African scholars in Djenne founded flourishing universities where they taught students, consulted their libraries, and composed learned treatises on Moslem science and philosophy. At the same time, they maintained close contacts with Islamic centers of learning across the Sahara. Such universities functioned not only as preservers and purveyors of the new culture, but also as centers for its dissemination still farther into the interior of Africa.

Early Literature

Students trained in the Islamic tradition and Arabic language produced black Africa's first written literature. Relatively little is known, as yet, about early Afro-Arabic writing, but the few examples we have indicate that it must have been a large literature. A seventh-century Afro-Arabic poet, Antar, for example, was represented in the oldest extant anthology of Arabic poetry, the *Golden Odes*. Antar inspired a whole school of writers called the Antarists whose works were collected around 800 by the famous Arab philologist Asma'i. Several Arabic poets of African origin, called "Arabic crows," won considerable reputations in the eighth century. Abu Dulama resided at the Caliph's court in Baghdad; Nusayb, perhaps the most gifted, lived in both Arabia and Egypt. Ibn al-Musajjih traveled widely over the Islamic world; and still another, Ziryab, was at the court of the most powerful Moslem ruler of the ninth century, the Caliph of Cordoba in Spain. Some early scholars also worked in Ge'ez and Amharic, the old languages of Ethiopia, particularly in translating Christian works from European languages. In more recent times a considerable literature has been written in Hausa, Swahili, and Malagasy, all languages influenced greatly by Arabic, and less successfully in Vai, the language of Liberia.

The bulk of black Africa's literature, however, was not written but oral, transmitted for centuries from generation to generation solely by word of mouth. Only recently has the work of collecting and transcribing this rich heritage of folk literature really begun. Just as black Africa's history was preserved in traditional oral archives, its wisdom and ethics—indeed, what we would today call its entire educational curriculum—was preserved in a tradition of oral literature. Listening repeatedly to recitations of songs, stories, legends, poems and proverbs, the young received their instruction not only in cosmogony, religious beliefs, moral values and history, but in social laws, political ideals, and practical economics as well. Before we explore African economics and politics, however, a brief look at Medieval Europe will provide a helpful contrast.

Land, Labor, and Power in Medieval Europe

Medieval Europe's agriculture, like its settlement patterns, also bore a heavy Roman imprint. In Romanized parts of Europe, agriculture had been organized largely in terms of slave or servile labor on huge estates called latifundia or villas, and farming techniques were typically intensive. Faced with limited amounts of cultivable soil, which at best was light and thin, and a climate characterized by dramatic changes from winter wetness to summer dryness, Roman farmers had early devised solutions to these problems that were effective but demanded careful and constant labor. They had to keep their land clean and lightly ploughed during the winter season so that it would soak up the heavy downpours and, at the same time, drain off excess water that might erode the topsoil or rot their young seedlings. After their crops were harvested and the summer heat had lessened, they cleared their field by burning and ploughing. The field was allowed to lie fallow the following season to regain its fertility, but even then it was frequently ploughed to keep it clean of all weeds that might use up the precious moisture. Only such laborious dry-farming techniques, supplemented in some areas with equally intensive irrigated farming, enabled ancient growers to make profitable use of their marginal soils.

After the collapse of the Empire in western Europe, both the pattern of estate organization and the techniques of intensive cultivation, at least in the Romanized areas, were carried, with modifications, over into the early Middle Ages. By the fifth century, various Germanic groups had established kingdoms amid the decay of the Empire; they were already accustomed to Roman farming organization and techniques, and they simply continued them. Germans had been brought in first as slaves, workers and servants, then as soldiers, and later as officers and officials. Finally, some also became landlords in the Roman tradition.

As the centuries passed, German and Roman cultures mingled and merged and the distinction between the two disappeared. But the agricultural tradition remained basically intact. Villas, though they tended to become more isolated and self-sufficient, remained large, closely managed, and intensively cultivated. The introduction of a heavy moldboard plough enabled the inhabitants to work the heavy clay soils of the north European Plain, a largely un-Romanized area, on which the light scratch ploughs used in the Mediterranean lands had proved worthless. Vast areas of lowland forests were transformed into fertile fields. Indeed, the period between the eleventh and thirteenth centuries has been aptly called the Great Age of Clearing, as improved agriculture spread over the continent. Even so, for most medieval men, whether serf, peasant, townsman or even nobleman, poverty was an ever present companion. Most people rarely had enough bread or porridge (oats, peas, or beans) to eat, much less meat, for land was too scarce to use for fodder crops. The yield was pitifully small in medieval fields—three to five bushels of grain for each bushel sowed. (The modern yield is something like twenty to one.) What blight and marauding armies did not destroy in the fields, insects, rodents, rot or fire frequently got in the storerooms. In times of stress—war, drought, or pestilence—poverty became serious deprivation. Not infrequently large numbers of people died of complications brought on by malnutrition or from outright starvation.

Agricultural Slavery

The typical agricultural laborer on Medieval manors, at least in most of western Europe, was not a slave as he had been under the Romans, but a serf. In other words, he was not legally owned, but in practice he was inextricably bound and committed to the person on whose land he lived and worked. The decline of slavery and the subsequent rise of serfdom in many areas was one of the most striking changes to occur in early Medieval Europe. In late Republican and early Imperial Roman times the growth of large-scale industrial and commercial enterprises, increased wealth, and the growth of great latifundia, particularly in Italy and Sicily, led to a dramatic expansion of agricultural slavery. Rome's almost constant wars during the last two centuries of the Republic furnished a constant and cheap supply of war captives from around the Mediterranean, though almost no slaves as yet came from black Africa. Some slaves were trained as gladiators, while many more were sent to the mines.

But by far the greatest number went to the fields. The tremendous increase in agricultural slavery during the Roman period represented a marked change in the history of both farming and slavery. Before that time, most farming had been done on small, individually owned and worked plots on which slave labor was of little profit. The Roman aristocracy, however, grown rich from exploitation of the empire, invested in huge tracts of land on which they found slave labor most useful. Such owners developed a system of gang labor, professional management, and absentee ownership that in many respects resembled the later plantation system of the Americas. The large estate made slave labor profitable in all types of agricultural enterprise—grain, wine, olive, cattle—and masters carefully sought out slaves who had the particular skills that their estate needed at the time; Thracians and Illyrians were famous as herdsmen, and Greeks and Syrians for olive and wine culture.

The legal status of slaves was set in ancient times. The slave was a chattel, a piece of movable property that could be bought, sold, traded, leased, mortgaged, bequeathed, given away, or seized in bankruptcy. But he could not be destroyed at will, for he was also recognized as a person, and as such was afforded limited rights and protection. An owner could punish a slave and even mark him by branding or tatooing, but he could not, legally, do him severe bodily harm or kill him. Provisions for manumission and the legal status of offspring of slaves were carefully defined in the law codes. Many of the legal characteristics of bondage as set in the ancient world remained unchanged in western civilization for more than three thousand years. Ancient slavery was distinguished most strikingly from the later New World slavery by the fact that ancient slavery was never based on race. More often than not slaves in the ancient Mediterranean world were of stock very similar to their masters.

The increasing number of slaves employed on Roman latifundia under constantly deteriorating living conditions led inevitably to revolts. Slave uprisings occurred with increasing regularity and ferocity from the opening of the second century B.C. onward. In spite of constant vigilance and periodic purges of troublemakers from among the slave population, bloody revolts continued. In the most famous revolt of all, the slave gladiator Spartacus in 73-71 B.C., with ninety thousand fellow gladiators, slaves and desperados, plundered and terrorized the whole of Italy before being defeated and killed. As a result of such revolts Rome developed pervasive fear and harsh militancy, responses similar to those made many centuries later by the West Indies and the American South to their own slave and ex-slave problems.

Slavery's Decline

The decline of slavery in Europe, already in progress during the latter centuries of the Roman Empire and not complete until well into the High Middle Ages, was gradual, piecemeal, and extremely complex. But we can at least sketch something of its outline and note some of the causes behind it. Slavery had traditionally proved profitable only when conditions afforded certain requirements: constant replenishing of the slave labor force with new purchases (for natural breeding on a given estate never furnished an adequate supply), careful provisioning of slaves with food, clothing, shelter, etc., close overseeing and control, and exact estate management. Late Imperial and early Medieval conditions in much of Europe militated against all of these.

Slavery continued, however, substantially as it existed in Roman times, in peripheral areas of the continent such as the Iberian peninsula and eastern Europe. On the Iberian peninsula, wars between Christian and Moslems kept the institution alive by supplying Moslem captives for the slave market. On the other side of Europe, Kievan princes in Russia continued to send slaves, drawn from their own or neighboring populations, to the East in exchange for silks and spices. And Italian slave merchants, particularly Venetians, transported slaves drawn from the Slavic populations around the Black and Adriatic Seas—whence derived the European word "slave"—to harems and households in Syria, Egypt, and occasionally Italy and Spain.

In the rest of Europe the decline of slavery was hastened by a number of factors. Though the wars between Romans and barbarians in the latter days of the Empire furnished some captives for the slave markets (but by no means as many as the earlier wars of expansion during the Republic), the general economic depression that plagued the west had so fiscally crippled most landlords that they were unable to purchase the needed slaves. And Christianity, though it did not proscribe slavery as such or even the holding of Christians as slaves, did resolutely forbid the enslavement of anyone already a Christian. As a result, new slaves had to be brought from faraway non-Christian areas—Moslem North Africa, the Slavic lands around the Black Sea, the pagan Baltic, and the primitive northwestern fringes of Europe. Thus the supply of slaves, though constant, was insufficient to maintain a great servile economy. Moreover, the general ignorance, disorder and distress that the opening of the Middle Ages brought made estate management, provisioning and overseeing more and more difficult. A slave estate required sophisticated management, for it was based on a delicate balance of exchange, consumption, and profit. Hundreds of people had to be provided for out of the produce of the fields, a reserve set aside, the remainder sold, and a profit margin maintained. All this required that careful accounts be kept. Such elaborate enterprises proved too much for the average administrators of the early medieval period to handle. Similarly, the sheer size of estates plus a lack of trained personnel made the problems of adequate overseeing and direction of the estate increasingly difficult. Even the estate owners themselves, now primarily soldiers by training rather than aristocratic Roman agriculturalists, were more times than not at a loss as to where to turn or what to do.

The problem was how to replace slaves with a readily available, easy to manage, and cheap labor supply. The answer was serfdom. Masters began to turn their slaves into dependent tenants by assigning families the responsibilities for cultivating specific plots of land. Families thus "hutted," that is assigned a hut and land, could themselves farm their plot with minimum supervision and divide the excess produce with the master. Though such tenants long remained legally slaves, gradually that designation disappeared. Even by the late fourth century, Roman law, with an eye on a new class of taxpayers, expressly forbade the sale or forceable eviction of rural slaves whose names were on the tax rolls as tenant farmers. The pattern was set: once a farmer, always a farmer.

As the centuries passed, the obligations as well as the rights of tenant farmers became fixed by custom and law, and their designation as slaves was effaced. By around the eleventh century they had become what we commonly call serfs. During the same centuries that slaves were becoming serfs, free peasants of the Roman Empire underwent a similar transformation. Originally free peasants were of two general types: those who worked as free farm laborers (coloni) on lands belonging to a landlord and those who owned their own farms outright. The former group, like the "hutted" slaves, were early bound to the soil by imperial legislation. Though they were legally "free," that is, not belonging in their person to anyone, their status gradually became, for practical purposes, indistinguishable from the slaves who had been made into dependent tenants or serfs. The second group, those who owned their own land, suffered a slightly different fate. Many of them, losing their lands in times of economic crisis, passed over into tenancy as a matter of course. Others retained their lands, their fields more often than not mixed up with those of adjacent tenancies, only to be engulfed—sometimes after centuries of precarious independence—by the new system that so completely surrounded and dominated them. In many cases the awareness of the distinction between their status and that of their tenant neighbors was simply eroded by time and the passage of generations. Yet some, either by luck or stubborn persistence, survived the Middle Ages in control of their free or allodial lands.

The Seigniors

As laborers and small land owners changed into serfs, their former leaders, employers, or masters developed into a dominant, landholding, warrior class—seigniors or lords. Serfs, whatever their precise legal status, did not work for themselves alone; a great part of their toil went towards the maintenance of their lord. To the lord the serfs owed a considerable portion of their time—a specified number of days of labor in his fields, meadows, or vineyards, as well as certain carrying services, and sometimes their labor as repairmen, builders, or craftsmen. Further they were obliged to give over to him for his use a sizable part of their harvests, sometimes in the form of rents paid in kind and sometimes in the form of taxes paid in money. Moreover lords, holding the lands that the serfs worked and more often than not the villages in which they lived, were protectors, judges, and governors. Thus the seigniory or manor was not simply an economic enterprise; it was a unit of political authority as well.

The exact origins of seigniory are as obscure as those of serfdom, but some of the lines along which it developed can be discerned. One source from which seigniory seems to have derived was ancient chieftainship. We have some scanty evidence to indicate that there existed in ancient Celtic and Germanic societies a recognized leadership class to whom deference and certain services were traditionally accorded. Most scholars think it likely that, in some cases at least, this caste persevered to be transformed gradually into feudal nobles. Another source of seigniory was the practice of "hutting" already described. The late Roman and early Medieval villa owners who settled their slaves as tenants simply continued to extract labor services and a share of the harvest from them as payment for use of the land. Still another, and perhaps the most common, origin of lordship was simple force. An individual, growing richer than his neighbors by luck or skill, was able to surround himself with armed followers and dominate his village and the surrounding countryside. Such a person thus established for his family a dominance, or what came to be called lordship.

The Fighting Class: Nobles and Kings

During the same centuries that the institution of seigniory was establishing the relationship between Europe's landholding warriors and its landworking serfs that was to endure for a thousand years or more, another institution, that commonly called feudalism, was slowly but surely establishing distinctions in rank as well as defining relationships among the warriors or nobles themselves. In some cases feudal relationships were, like serfdom and seigniory, traceable to the old villa system. The villa owners who had converted their slaves into tenants in order to escape the heavy cost of maintaining them directly soon discovered that they could apply the same principle to the problem of providing for their military retainers too. Instead of continuing to feed, house and equip their ever more expensive private armies from their own pockets, villa owners began granting each fighting man control of a portion of the villa lands, including the tenants living thereon. Military retainers were thus turned into professional military class so that they might support themselves, or more precisely, so that their tenants might support them. The fighting men remained subservient, at least partially, to their benefactors. They recognized him as their overlord or suzerain and, in return for the grants of land and tenants, continued, as vassals, to serve him as soldiers, or in special cases as advisors, members of his court, and sometimes as administrators.

There is evidence to indicate that in other cases remnants of ancient tradition afforded nobles who were recognized or presumed descendants of Celtics or German chiefs opportunities for establishing themselves as overlords of less well-pledged nobles. Such cases must have been relatively few however, for as important as tradition was during those troubled centuries, force proved a much more powerful argument. More often than not the richest and strongest nobleman in an area, regardless of his ancestry, won from his fellow nobles recognition as their overlord. In some cases he might have gained such recognition through merit, but in most cases he forced his neighbor to succumb to his threats of reprisal. Such vassal-overlord relationships were, by around 1000, widespread in central and western Europe. They linked most of the warrior classes, who were the rich and powerful landed nobility of the continent, together in a network of mutual personal prerogatives and obligations.

In the absence of strong central authority, which had disappeared in the West with the collapsed Roman empire, such personal ties among the powerful warrior class functioned as a system of governance. In time, a feudal hierarchy developed; overlords in a region fell under the sway of even more powerful lords, usually one of their own number, and became his vassal, responsible for serving him in much the same way that their own vassals served them. At the top of the feudal pyramid sat the king, who was the suzerain or overlord, at least in theory, of even the most powerful. At each level of the pyramid, suzerains performed the necessary functions of government—calling up armies of vassals in time of war, administering justice, and collecting the necessary monies to pay for such services.

Military service was the basic obligation of a vassal to his lord. If the lord's lands were invaded by an enemy, his vassals were bound to come to his aid as fighting knights. In addition, vassals were often expected to garrison any fortresses that their lord might maintain, and in some cases they had to act as guards or retainers in the lord's own castle. Service in an overlord's court was next in importance to service in his army. At court, disagreements between vassals as well as disputes between vassals and the lord himself were settled, all vassals sitting in judgement as peers or equals. Such assemblages of vassals also counseled their lord on important matters such as military campaigns, changes in regulations or procedures regarding the conduct of affairs in general, and the marriages of the lord's children—a thing of no little importance in an age so dependent upon the workings of interpersonal relationships.

Vassals also had certain economic obligations to their suzerains. When a lord died, his vassals made a "relief" payment to his heir and successor, and when a vassal died, his own heir made a similar payment. Originally designed to insure that the vassalage would be renewed, such payments became customary and continued to be paid for centuries after the inheritance of such rights became, in practice, automatic. If the lord needed assistance—for example, when he was captured in war, when he planned a costly crusade or pilgrimage, when his eldest daughter was to be married or his eldest son initiated as a warrior, or knighted—it was incumbent upon his vassals to pay him "aids." Because money was scarce or nonexistent, most vassals made their payments in services.

Feudalism thus provided the fundamentals of governance, but only the bare fundamentals. The warrior class of nobles who dominated Europe tolerated only the minimum of restraining laws or customs. Crimes committed by vassals against their lord or fellow vassals were rigorously and barbarously punished, but crimes, even of the most heinous nature including murder, pillage, and rape, committed against vassals of another lord or against peasants and serfs were largely ignored.

Though the king was theoretically the suzerain of his entire realm, he was rarely very powerful during the early Medieval centuries. The nobles with the strongest castles, the best fortifications, the largest armies, and the greatest incomes, whatever their rank on the feudal scale, were the real powers. Kings were weak primarily because taxation in the modern sense—and, indeed, in the Roman sense—did not exist in the Middle Ages. Without a money economy, such taxes were impossible. Kings were almost totally dependent for income upon their own personal landholdings, a meager base for maintaining a government. Moreover, the independent-minded feudal nobility, always fearful of control from the crown, conscientiously and effectively undermined the efforts of the king to increase his authority. Virtually the sole role of the king for centuries was to call upon the nobles to defend the realm when it was threatened by invasion and to act as a ceremonial figurehead atop the feudal hierarchy.

The Divine Right of Kings

In spite of the obstacles, kings gradually managed to increase their power. They gained enormously from the introduction into Europe of the concept of divine kingship. First brought into the European world by Alexander the Great and perpetuated by the Roman emperors, the idea that the ruler was a living god to be obeyed without question or hesitation was handed on—only slightly altered by Christian thought—to Medieval Europe. In the Christian tradition the king was not a god, but a man singled out by God to rule his fellow men. The Medieval church insisted that kings were appointed by God, not merely to lead armies and act as the symbolic heads of state, but to keep peace and order, aid the weak, and, particularly, to protect the church. Churchmen convinced Christian Europe that kings were priestly figures, especially chosen by God. Nothing could have suited the purposes of the kings better. In large measure protected by their new cloak of sacrosanctity—they came to have themselves not only crowned, but anointed, and professed to have certain miraculous powers such as the "touch" to cure diseases—they found themselves in a position to begin an assault on the nobles.

Much of the political history of the High Middle Ages, the period between the eleventh and thirteenth centuries, is to be told in terms of the successes of monarchs in subduing feudal magnates and establishing increasing degrees of centralized royal authority. Taking advantage of the commercial revival that characterized these centuries and the subsequent increase in the supply of money in circulation, kings began to establish standing royal armies with which they could quell recalcitrant nobles and impose order on their kingdoms. At the same time they hired bureaucrats to staff their expanding governments, and trained judges to sit on the new royal courts they established to compete with local feudal courts. Some of the monarchs in western Europe were able to begin imposing direct and indirect taxes on their realms, thereby guaranteeing themselves resources that none of their vassals, even the mightiest, could hope to equal. Having subdued the feudal nobility by around 1300, some monarchs turned and attacked their former ally, the church. This final phase of the kings' struggle for complete control of their states, however, was eclipsed by the general crisis that engulfed all of Europe in the late Middle Ages.

But we shall return to that part of the story later; we now need to look at political developments in Africa south of the Sahara.

Black African Empires

States first developed in the interior of Africa along two axes, one running north-south from the upper Nile valley into the lake district, and the other east-west through the Sudan belt. The earliest non-Mediterranean states in Africa arose on the north-south axis, adjacent to ancient Egypt. Egyptians were carrying on a substantial trade in such materials as ebony, ivory, and animal skins with black Africa from as early as the third millennium B.C., and by the second millennium had pushed halfway up the Nile to colonize the gold-producing areas of

Nubia. Beyond Nubia, however, Egypt did not achieve dominance, for there the indigenous state of Kush emerged at the beginning of the first millennium B.C. The kingdom of Kush, though heavily influenced by Egyptian civilization, was to endure as an independent state on the upper Nile until the middle of the fourth century A.D., a period of more than a thousand years. The princes of Kush conquered the decadent Egyptian kingdom in the eighth century B.C. and ruled it as the Twenty-fifth Dynasty of Pharaohs, making their capital, Napata, for a time the center of the ancient world. When in the following century the Assyrians invaded Egypt, the Kushites abandoned it, retreated to their homeland, and began to push their frontiers southward into black Africa. They established a new capital at Meroe farther up the Nile; here they developed over the next several centuries a prosperous economy including a full-scale iron industry and a thriving trade with the Mediterranean and the Near East, as well as a rich culture which preserved much Egyptian religious and ceremonial tradition.

As the kingdom fell into poverty and weakness after the second century of the Christian era, however, a nearby commercial principality, Axum, began to rise. In the fourth century Axum, already Christianized, captured Meroe and crushed the whole kingdom of Kush, which had in its heyday, and perhaps even more so in its declining years, exerted tremendous influence on neighboring areas of the Sudan. Its influence was felt particularly on the areas to the southwest such as Dafur and perhaps even on the Kanem-Bornu states that grew up around Lake Chad. To the southeast Axum now began to lay the foundations of a new empire that would survive, in spite of many changes, into the twentieth century as modern Ethiopia.

Along the other axis, that running east-west through the Sudan belt and eventually extending down through the open savanna country of east-central Africa, another series of states arose, the histories of which are more germane to the story we are developing. These states emerged somewhat later and somewhat more independent of Egyptian influence than those on the north-south axis. These areas developed common characteristics of political organization sufficient to evidence what some modern historians call a "Sudanic" type of state.

In contrast to Medieval Europe where a chronic scarcity of cultivable land led to a feudal political system based directly on landholding, black Africa, never short of land and always underpopulated, developed a very different type of power base. Sudanic states were built on lineage systems and kinship groups such as families, tribes or clans. The key figures at the local level were family patriarchs, tribal elders and village chiefs who derived their authority from their inherited positions as heads of their groups. Tradition rigidly defined the status and function of each group, leaders, farmers, craftsmen, merchants, or religious figures. Kingship, both in its political and its associated ritual importance, was also defined by the lineage system. Royal lineages came into existence when a local chief, elder or renowned warrior gained dominance over neighboring communities; he then imposed his and his family's authority on that local group leaders, thereby creating a higher level of centralized power—the beginnings of a state—much as feudal lords and kings did in Medieval Europe. Sudanic political organization was thus something imposed from above rather than generated from below. As more and more villages were brought under control, the ruler, or king, became more and more a remote power figure who had to appoint officials to represent him in each locality—that is, to perform political and ritual functions in his stead. Such provincial officials along with several titled office holders immediately surrounding the king came to constitute a vast hierarchic bureaucracy that administered the royal government at the king's pleasure.

Sudanic states did not seek to impose any one particular civilization, religion, or cultural tradition upon the peoples within them. Hundreds, even thousands, of diverse societies and ethnic groups of varying dimensions and levels of development existed side by side under the rule of the royal master. One lineage, for example, might convert to Islam and develop a learned and sophisticated family tradition, while the other classes of the community remained pagans of one kind or another. Nor were these states based on territorial sovereignty, for land itself, in abundant supply, was of little significance; consequently they had no fixed frontiers. The Sudanic states were more spheres of influence defined not by territorial boundaries, but by the number and nature of socio-economic groups whom the ruler controlled and from whom he could exact labor, military and administrative service, and tribute.

Divine Rights of Kings in Black Africa

One of the chief characteristics of Sudanic civilization was the institution of divine kingship. So strikingly similar was the Sudanic manifestation of this idea to that of ancient Egypt that some modern scholars believe it likely that at least this element of Egyptian civilization some-how found its way from the interior of Africa into the Nile valley, though there is little positive evidence of its route of travel. Sudanic kings, claiming descent from mythological tribal heroes or conquerors, were believed to have supernatural powers over such things as the fertility of land, the regularity of rain, and the security of life in general. Because so much depended upon the physical well-being and happiness of the kings, divine honors were paid them. The kings lived apart from the population, virtually secluded in huge royal palaces equipped to feed and house the hundreds of officials and retainers who waited upon them. No one, not even an intimate, was allowed to see the god-kings take nourishment—they took their meals in complete privacy. More-over, when giving audiences, the kings were usually screened from public view and often communicated only indirectly through special court officials. Only the kings could perform special rituals to insure good harvests and perpetuation of the tribe, some of which involved sowing the first seeds at the right time of the moon and tending a perpetual flame, a symbol of continued life and prosperity. When kings died—and natural death, degrading for a divine personage, was often avoided by means of ritual poisoning or suffocation—their bodies were embalmed, honored with elaborate funerals involving animal and some-times human sacrifices, and entombed in royal mausoleums.

The royal funerals of the old empire of Ghana were described in the mid-eleventh century by the Moslem geographer, Al Bakri. When a king died, he wrote, a large dome of wood was built on the spot chosen for his tomb. Inside the dome the king's body was placed on a couch covered with carpets and cushions, and beside him were set his weapons, personal treasures, and the vessels from which he was accus-tomed to eat and drink, along with a plentiful supply of food. Then his personal servants, particularly those who had prepared his meals, were brought and sealed in the tomb with their master. Workers afterwards covered the whole dome with dirt to make a huge mound, dug a moat around it, and fashioned a bridge of earth and a formal approachway to the tomb.

The Earliest Empire: Ghana

The empire traditionally called Ghana, after the title of its ruler, was, as far as we know from present evidence, the earliest of the Sudanic states.

It rose at an uncertain date well before the eighth century, when it was first mentioned in Arabic sources, reached its peak in the middle of the eleventh, and declined rapidly in the twelfth century. It was an inland state in West Africa, occupying roughly the region between the Senegal and the Niger rivers, though including neither, and covering an area about the size of France and England combined. Ghana was fundamentally a commercial state, its power based on the immense wealth that its king and merchant class derived from their position as middlemen in the salt and gold trade. Arabic writers repeatedly referred to it during the centuries of its prosperity as the richest of all lands and one with extraordinarily wide commercial contacts. One writer in the mid-tenth century reported seeing in Morocco a Ghanaian merchant's check for 42,000 dinars ($280,000?)—a far larger check than he had ever seen in the great trading centers in Syria and Iraq.

The king of Ghana was able to tap the rich commerce for revenue to support his government. Although he did not control the gold mines, he did collect a heavy tax from the gold trade by claiming all gold nuggets as his own, leaving only gold dust for transshipment north. He also collected one dinar on every donkey load of salt that entered his kingdom and two dinars for every one that left, as well as similar imposts on copper and other trade goods. In addition the king exacted heavy tribute from several vassal kings and chiefs within his empire, holding their sons at his court as hostages. Considering the volume of trade that passed through Ghana and the size of the empire, the royal income must have been considerable. One evidence was the crown's rumored ability to put an army of 200,000 men in the field, 40,000 of whom were archers.

Though Islam spread widely throughout the Ghana empire during the centuries of its greatness, the kings themselves were never converted. They had, however, many Moslems in their service, even as ministers of state and advisors to the crown. Unfortunately for Ghana, the spread of Islam did not remain peaceful. In the 1040's a group of fanatical Moslems bent upon forcing conversions at the point of a sword—the Almoravids—sprang up among the Berbers in the Senegal region northwest of Ghana. The Almoravids not only attacked trans-Saharan caravans, but conquered and plundered several of Ghana's vassal states. For over thirty years the empire was embroiled in a series of wars and revolts that disrupted its trade, devastated its agriculture, depopulated its cities, and demoralized its government. Though it managed to recover its energies and some of its property and power early in the twelfth century, Ghana was henceforth only a shadow of its former self. It drifted into decline, suffered further defeats, and was reduced for a while to the status of a tributary state to Susa, one of its former dependencies. Finally in 1235 it was conquered and its capital city of Ghana razed by the armies of a new power, Mali.

Mali

Mali, destined to be richer and larger than Ghana, began as a small Mande, or Mandingo, chieftaincy near the junction of the Niger and Sankarani Rivers. By the tenth century its ruling family had solidified control over neighboring areas and began to construct a state. Moslems from the beginning, Mali's kings used to an advantage the literacy, adminstrative skill and statecraft associated with the Islamic faith. Their kingdom grew steadily in power and influence during the eleventh and twelfth centuries, expanded rapidly in the thirteenth, and reached its height in the first half of the fourteenth century. At its greatest extent the Mali empire, centered somewhat east of where the old Ghana empire had been, stretched from the headwaters and middle reaches of the Senegal and Gambia Rivers in the west, eastward along the course of the Niger for about half its length and as far south as the origins of the Niger, but not quite as far north as Ghana had extended. It was as large as Spain, Portugal, France and Italy together.

Larger and better situated than Ghana had been, Mali was able to reap even greater benefits. Ghana, centered in the area where the Sahara met the savanna country, had based her economy largely on commerce, while Mali, located in the very center of the savanna, could balance her commerce with substantial agriculture. Indeed, her kings always encouraged agricultural development, and one of them, Sundiata, early introduced the cultivation and processing of cotton. Moreover, the Mali empire contained the copper-producing region of Takedda and, more important, the gold producing areas of fabled Wangara, from which Ghana had profited but had not owned. Control of the gold sources meant that Mali's cities soon attracted the caravans from across the Sahara, and the empire grew even richer. Ibn Khaldun, the most famous of all Arabic historians, reported caravans of 12,000 camels traveling to

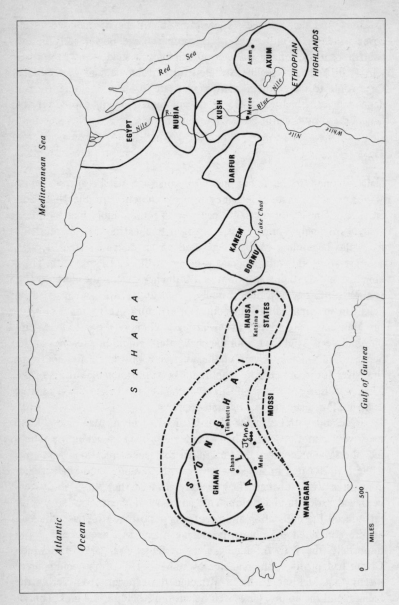

Africa's Ancient Empires

Mali in 1353. Though barter was still frequently practiced, cowrie shells developed into an extensively used medium of exchange throughout the Sudan. To share in the trans-Saharan trade as well as that on the Niger, Mali's kings built a capital city at Niani, north of the other three great commercial cities of the empire, Timbuktu, Djenne, and Gao.

As they conquered more and more areas, the kings of Mali, called Mansas, brought their realm effective administration by dividing it into provinces and placing an official in charge of each. There were over fourteen such provinces, most ruled by appointed governors or emirs, usually native generals, though some of the Berber areas were ruled through their own local sheiks. In addition the more important cities had special crown-appointed administrative officials called farbas. Some officials were given fiefs in exchange for their services; others were paid salaries. All were subject to the direction of the king who acted through his court bureaucracy. At his court the king not only required the customary elaborate ceremony and ritual surrounding his person, but also vested deserving state servants with titles and honors such as the famous Order of the Trousers which entitled its holders to wear large baggy trousers as special insignia. The Mali kings also maintained close and friendly diplomatic relations with other African states, especially with the sultans of Morocco and Egypt, and insured their international prestige as well as their local power with a standing army said to be 100,000 strong. Financial support for the government came principally from imperial taxes on local crops and livestock and duties on commerce, supplemented by income from the king's personal agricultural holding and tribute from his vassals.

Of all the kings of Mali—and we know something of a great many of them, principally from Arabic sources—the greatest was Mansa Musa who ruled from 1302 to 1337, during the empire's height. Perhaps his most impressive work was in establishing peace and order; one Arab traveler later reported that there was "complete security in their country; neither traveler, nor inhabitant need fear anything from robbers or men of violence." In addition he was active in promoting agriculture, commerce, education and refurbishing cities; he built for himself, for example, a great brick palace with a plastered dome and painted walls. Mansa Musa, a devout Moslem, also took an active role in reforming, strengthening and propagating Islam throughout his realm. In fact, it was his religious pilgrimage through Cairo to Mecca in 1324-25 that literally put Mali on the maps. The kings of Mali had all traditionally made similar pilgrimages to the holy sanctuary in Mecca, but none had ever before undertaken one on such a scale. Mansa Musa left Mali with between 80 and 100 camel loads of gold, five hundred slaves, and an enormous entourage of personal retainers. The Arab historian Al Umari wrote that Mansa Musa gave away so much gold in Cairo—not a single royal office holder was left without a gift of gold, he said—that the gold market there was glutted and the price of the precious metal fell drastically, endangering the entire Egyptian economy.

After Mansa Musa's death the empire continued to flourish for another two decades, but decline set in after 1350, perhaps brought on, certainly aggravated, by attacks from neighboring principalities and by internal revolts, civil wars and palace revolutions. In weakened condition the aging empire was easy prey for a new and vigorous state that was rising, Songhai.

Songhai

Songhai, centered still farther east than either Ghana or Mali, eventually included all the territories of both its predecessors and much more besides. Like Mali, it had fertile agricultural and grazing lands to which the benefits of profitable trade were added, especially towards the end of the ninth century when its capital of Gao became a major terminus of trans-Saharan commercial routes. For several centuries it remained a small but rich principality, a vassal state under Mali domination. Around 1375 it took advantage of the decay and disintegration of the Mali empire, broke away, and maintained a precarious independence until 1468. In that year Sunni Ali ascended the throne of the little state and within twenty-eight years had transformed it into an empire.

Sunni Ali was a man of action without time or sympathy for cultural or religious refinements. A pagan, he ruthlessly crushed any opposition to his state-building plans, whether it came from obstinate tribesmen or learned Moslem scholars. He organized an army of cavalry and infantry, complemented it with a fleet of ships on the Niger and set out on a remarkable career of conquest. He wrested the rich city of Timbuktu from the Tuaregs who had taken it, absorbed remnants of the Mali empire including Djenne, seized lands bordering the Mossi tribes, and marched east annexing everything between Gao and the Hausa states. His conquests completed, he began organizing his new subjects along the lines of the old Mali administration, appointing governors over some newly created provinces and maintaining local rulers as tribute-paying vassals in other areas. Sunni Ali's conquests and administrative consolidations laid the foundations for the Songhai empire.

Mohammed Askia, Sunni Ali's prime minister, seized the throne upon his master's death in 1493 and held it until 1528, founding a new dynasty that would rule the empire for the rest of its history. To strengthen his hold on the throne, Mohammed Askia exiled or executed the legitimate heirs of Sunni Ali and assiduously cultivated the influential Moslem elements of the population whom Sunni Ali had antagonized. Already a Moslem himself, Mohammed Askia ostentatiously undertook a pilgrimage to Mecca which surpassed in richness the famous one made earlier by Mansa Musa, and returned from his trip bearing an impressive title awarded him by the Moslem leaders of the east, Caliph of the Blacks. His crown secured, he turned to conquest, and by the end of his reign the Songhai state controlled all territory from the middle reaches of the Senegal and Gambia Rivers in the west to the Hausa states in the east, and from the salt-mining center of Taghaza in the Sahara to the borders of the Mossi kingdom in the south, an area larger than the ancient Roman Empire in Europe.

Next, Mohammed Askia set about devising a more effective means of governing his enormously enlarged empire. He abolished the old system of provincial administration, redivided the realm into four great units, over each of which he placed a director general. Each of these four divisions was in turn subdivided into provinces, each with its own governor. At the same time he established a system of courts for administering justice, based on Islamic law, in the larger towns and cities throughout his domain. Immediately around himself he created a council consisting of his chief general, his commander of the fleet, his chief tax-collector, his chief diplomat, the manager of his estates, and the official who policed rivers, lakes and waterways. The king filled the main offices in his bureaucracy with members of his own family, hoping thereby to insure not only firm support for his policies but the perpetuation of his lineage in power as well.

To finance his government, Mohammed Askia used slave labor on the royal estates to produce foodstuffs, mainly grains and dried fish, and weapons such as swords, spears, bows and arrows. Most of this production went to support the king's staff and army, but any surplus was sold for profit. In addition the king obtained revenue from the customary taxes on agriculture and from tribute dues, but most important was the income derived from trade—customs duties, tolls, and fees. Recognizing the importance of this source of money, the king did everything he could to encourage and protect commerce. Like contemporary monarchs in Western Europe, he protected and patronized his great cities—Timbuktu, Djenne, and Gao; he encouraged the use of money and perhaps coined it; he certainly used his army to patrol and protect caravan routes; he worked to standardize weights and measures; and he employed royal inspectors to police markets and report infractions of commercial laws. Trade boomed and royal revenues grew apace.

After reaching its zenith in the first three decades of the sixteenth century, the Songhai empire fell into troubled times. In the several decades that followed, struggles for the throne, palace revolutions and inept government marred the image of the kingship and threatened the economic and political stability of the realm as a whole. The empire remained intact, even prosperous, however. Then suddenly and unexpectedly the end came—in the form of a lightning invasion from Morocco. In 1591 four thousand troops of the Sultan of Morocco carrying firearms met 27,000 Songhai warriors carrying only spears, swords, clubs, bows and arrows. The Songhai forces were completely routed, Gao was occupied, Timbuktu sacked, and the empire collapsed, never to revive. What remained became a languishing Moroccan province.

Eastern Kingdoms

As the Niger region of the Sudan fell into economic stagnation and political disorder following the Moroccan conquest, the way was opened for the development of areas farther east. The Hausa states, seven in number, lying about halfway between the Niger and the older Kanem-Bornu states around Lake Chad were the principal beneficiaries. Though relatively little is yet known about the origins of these states, scholars generally agree that, though these peoples had lived there for centuries, probably in unorganized family groups, it was not until at least the fourteenth century that they became in any way significant. There is no evidence that before that time they traded with their black neighbors or with the Moslems across the desert. Gradually, however, they began to develop both political and economic organization, and by the end of the fifteenth century were full grown states with wide commercial contacts not only with the trans-Saharan and the Songhai empire, but with the far away rain forest areas of the west coast as well. The flourishing new Hausa states attracted considerable numbers of merchants, scholars and administrators from the wreckage of the Songhai empire in the late sixteenth and seventeenth centuries, thereby adding to their luster and prosperity. The city of Katsina with a population of around 100,000, capital of the state of the same name, was the most important center in the Sudan in the seventeenth and eighteenth centuries.

The Dominance of the Atlantic Frontier

Katsina, however, would never develop into an empire. Its future was already sealed, as for that matter, was the future of most of Africa. African history, during the centuries that we have followed it thus far, was the story of the great empires of the interior of the continent. From the beginning, they were oriented to the Mediterranean world and largely dependent upon the trans-Saharan trade with Mediterranean markets. However, all that was changed by the opening of the Atlantic at the end of the fifteenth century. The Ocean Sea at that point began to replace the Mediterranean as the economic and political focus of Europe and Africa. The European states fortunate enough to lie on the north Atlantic seashores reaped rich benefits from the shift away from the Mediterranean coasts. In Africa a startlingly similar shift of focus took place. As the old empires located in the interior reaches of the Sudan declined, new areas hitherto isolated, relatively underpopulated and underdeveloped—the rain forest kingdoms on the Atlantic coast— began their ascent. These kingdoms, like their counterparts in western Europe, were oriented to the Atlantic and were to be deeply involved in its history; indeed, they were reluctant partners of western Europeans in its development and exploitation. Before we describe such developments, however, we must examine the commerce, the cities and the growing economic problems of Medieval Europe and Africa.

CHAPTER THREE

Commercial Contours of Africa and Europe

One of the striking similarities in the early histories of Africa and Europe is the role that extensive trade played in the development of the two continents. From ancient times on, goods (sometimes including slaves) and news of technological innovations flowed back and forth along a series of trade routes radiating from the Mediterranean through both continents. Long-distance trade nourished the growth of towns and cities that became the centers of wealth and power that, in Europe at least, fostered new drives that led to the discovery of the New World and transferred the focus of world commerce from the Mediterranean to the Atlantic.

African Technology and Trade

The economy of black Africa was far better developed in

ancient times than that of Europe beyond the Mediterranean orbit, and at least as well developed during much of medieval times as that of virtually any part of Europe. During those many centuries the basis of Africa's, as well as Europe's economy and civilization was agriculture. We have already noted the development of agriculture in the African savanna, and in a later chapter we shall return to the problems involved in introducing agriculture to the humid and overgrown forests of the Guinea coast, the Congo basin and the east central African lowlands. For the moment let us move on to other aspects of that continent's economy.

After agriculture, the next most important development in sub-Saharan Africa was ironworking. Gold and tin, both easily obtainable in relatively pure form from stream beds by washing, were known and used in Africa since pre-Roman times. Iron, however, had first to be mined, and then smelted. The fact that West Africa had no Bronze Age and practically no Copper Age in which techniques of smelting might have been developed, coupled with the fact that very few African Iron Age sites have as yet been excavated, complicates the problem of dating the origins of ironworking in the Sub-Sahara. Isolated recent finds imply that iron implements, possibly got by trade, were present in West Africa before 1100 B.C., but more general evidence indicates that such weapons and tools were not prevalent before 400 B.C. in the lake district of east-central Africa or before 300 B.C. in West Africa. The third century B.C. Nok culture that flourished in a 60,000-square-mile area of what is now central Nigeria left iron axes and slag heaps, suggesting that Africans were at that time smelting iron themselves. The origin of ironworking in Africa, like most questions in African history, is open to debate, but most authorities believe that the technology was diffused on a large scale perhaps in the third and second centuries B.C., from the Nile valley southward throughout the lake district and westward across the savanna belt to the Atlantic coast.

In Africa, as in other parts of the world, ironworking was a forest industry, dependent upon a ready and plentiful supply of wood fuel for the smelting process. This fact determined that its fullest development would occur not in the open part of the savanna, but in its wooded southern fringe and in the forests farther south. As Negroes from the Sudan belt penetrated the forests, occupied previously only by the primitive pygmies, they carried with them both their ironworking technology and their advanced agriculture. The former was as necessary for subduing the jungle as the latter was for using the cleared land profitably. The most southerly Negroes, the Bantu, living in the Cameroon highlands, advanced first into the rain forest as their population increased, perhaps around the third century B.C., spreading their numbers, their crops and their metallurgical skills not only through the Congo basin but across the savanna land south of it and into east-coastal Africa by perhaps the sixth century A.D. Similarly, Negroes from the western Sudan pushed southward into the forests along the Gulf of Guinea, carrying their civilization with them. Long before white explorers arrived on the coast in the 1400's, the Negroes had there developed a flourishing agricultural economy.

The early contacts between the Negroes of West Africa and their neighbors to the north across the Sahara (the Egyptians, Carthaginians, Romans, and particularly the Berbers) grew into a rich trade which, complementing agriculture, became the second basic element in the economic life of sub-Saharan Africa. Contacts existed from immemorial times, as distant perhaps as the fifth or sixth millennia B.C., as evidenced by the deep footpaths worn into the bedrock of the desert. Contacts had become frequent by the first millennium B.C., and regular enough by the fifth century B.C. to be fairly termed trade. The trans-Saharan commerce prospered in Roman times and flourished under Moslem influence from the sixth to the seventeenth century A.D.

Goods were carried for centuries by human bearers, then by horses and donkeys until the gradual desiccation made the desert impassable for them, and finally by camels which were introduced at the start of the Christian era. Negotiating the Sahara was never easy, even before climatic changes made it virtually impossible to live in. Nonetheless, over the centuries, the desert became literally criss-crossed with caravan routes. The four principal ones after about 1000 A.D. connected Timbuktu in the middle Niger with what is modern Morocco, the Hausa states in what is now northern Nigeria with ancient Carthage (modern Tunisia), the Kanem region near Lake Chad with Libya, and the central Sudan (modern Dafur) with ancient Egypt. Thus the entire Sudan belt remained in constant, if not easy, contact with the Mediterranean world.

Of the varied goods transported across the Sahara, including seeds, tools, weapons, glass beads, grain, dates and olives, the most important were salt and gold. Salt, a much desired flavoring and a much needed preservative, was unavailable in sub-Saharan Africa except by dangerous transport through the jungles from the Atlantic coast or by slow and inefficient distillation of grasses. The central Sahara, on the other hand, has a plentiful supply of it, and Berber traders made it readily available, at a price, to their southern neighbors. The goods from the north were exchanged for ivory, kola nuts, cotton, hides, some slaves, and particularly gold.

No one is certain of the location of the fabulous ancient gold mines of West Africa, but they were probably in what is now French Guinea, near the source of the Niger River. The Sudan Negroes who bartered gold to the Berbers for salt did not themselves mine the precious metal, but in turn traded for it with remote tribes farther south who controlled the mines. Much of the gold in the Ancient Near Eastern and Mediterranean worlds and of Medieval Europe came, via the Saharan trade routes, from one part of Africa or another. The Greek historian Herodotus, writing in the fifth century B.C., described how Carthaginian merchants bartered goods for gold with the natives on the African coast, each group placing what they had to offer on the beach and each silently adding to or taking away portions of it until an acceptable bargain was struck. As late as the seventeenth century the most famous of all English coins was struck in West African gold for the use of the Company of Royal Adventurers trading with Africa and was named the "Guinea."

In addition to the northern trade across the Sahara that the Sudanese states enjoyed, they also cultivated commercial contacts to the south, with the peoples living near the Guinea coast. There, merchants from both the western Sudan and from the Hausa states in the central Sudan held regularly scheduled markets or commercial fairs. In these markets the Sudan Negroes exchanged Saharan and trans-Saharan goods—particularly salt—along with some of their own—leather, for example—for the kola nuts and gold that they would later send north. Thus Sudanese traders, acting as middlemen, developed a network of trade routes linking the interior of Africa with the southern coastal region as well as with the mediterranean area.

African Cities

The extensive and lucrative Sudan trade was centered in black African cities. Indeed, the whole agrarian-based civilization of the Sudan, not

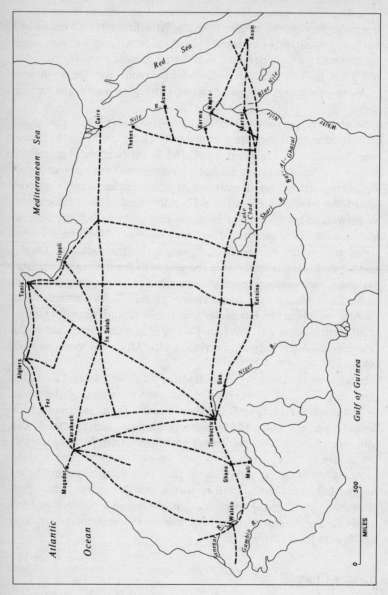

Major Trans-Saharan Empires

unlike that of contemporary Medieval Europe to the north, was concentrated in villages and towns. African farmers, like medieval serfs and peasants, lived not on the lands they worked, but in villages and towns whence they ventured each morning to till their fields and to which they returned at night for the security and protection of the settlement. Some of these communities, nourished by trade, grew into cities. Ghana, for example, the capital of the ancient empire of the same name, was described in its heyday, around 1050 A.D., by the famous Moslem geographer Al Bakri, who had heard of its wonders as far away as Spain. He wrote that the city of Ghana consisted of two main centers connected by some six miles of residential area. At one end was a kind of administrative area containing the king's palace, a fortress-like structure on the riverbank with painted walls, glass windows, and a defensive wall. In this part of the city also stood a domed pavilion used as a court of justice, a mosque, a prison, the royal tombs, and various statues and sacred groves. Some of the buildings were of stone, some of wood. The other end of the city formed a commercial center where most of the merchants, officials, scholars and foreigners lived. It contained twelve mosques, many markets, several wells, and numerous gardens. We have no information on the size of Ghana, but a Moslem observer in the 990's estimated that Awdaghost, a provincial town in the empire, had 300,000 households and a population of two million. This is obviously a gross exaggeration but gives some indication of how impressive the cities appeared to travelers.

Similarly, the fabled city of Timbuktu, which was founded around 1200 as a town of mud huts enclosed by a low mud wall, grew in prosperity and population to become a great city by the sixteenth century. At that time it was described by another famous European traveler, Leo Africanus, also of Spain, as an exceedingly rich city filled with shops and markets, and having many artisans and merchants, as well as judges, priests, officials, scholars and foreigners. The neighboring city of Djenne, even today one of the architectural marvels of the continent, was surrounded by a huge moat fashioned by connecting natural bodies of water with a network of artificial waterways to form an easy means of transportation as well as an effective defense against attack. Farther to the east, about half way between the Niger and the Nile, in modern Dafur, lay the empires of Kanem and Bornu, which rose in the tenth century and lasted until the nineteenth. The ruins scattered throughout this area suggest large ancient cities, such as the one at Jebel Uri, built of stone and gypsum, encircled by elaborate protective walls, and containing long causeways, houses, halls, and palaces. And southwards towards the end of east-central Africa's lake district, in modern Rhodesia, stand the impressive eleventh century stone ruins of Zimbabwe. Like the stone used in Dafur, those at Zimbabwe are neither trimmed square nor bound with mortar, but are fitted precisely together. These ruins are all that remain of what must have been the capital of a large and well organized black state thriving on a rich gold and ivory trade via the Indian Ocean.

Such African cities must have been in population, wealth, trade, administration and appearance comparable to European cities of the same period. Indeed, a Dutch traveler in 1602 compared the city of Benin, near the Guinea coast, with Amsterdam, one of the most advanced cities in Europe. To him Benin appeared "very large" with a great central avenue over four miles in length and "many times broader than the widest street in Amsterdam." The city was surrounded by a moat and an earthwork bulwark with gates of entry onto the main avenue. Outside the wall lay a great suburb. The houses within the city stood, he said, "as houses in Holland stand," close together fronting directly on the street, and had inside four large rooms plus kitchens as well as other storage and work rooms. The streets, like most streets in European cities of the time, were not paved. Perhaps the characteristic of African cities that contrasted most sharply with their counterparts in Europe lay in the kinds of building materials used. Medieval Europeans used large amounts of stone and kiln-dried brick along with wood and thatch. Africans had little stone at their disposal. They had to rely largely on wood, on a primitive cement obtained from anthills, on sun-dried brick, and on mud stucco. Such materials limited not only the size and complexity of buildings, but also their durability, for these materials deteriorated rapidly under attacks of insects and humidity.

The urban communities in Africa, as elsewhere in the world, became the focus of social structures and the nucleus of political systems. The simple village usually represented a single basic kinship unit with virtually all of its members engaged in farming. Larger towns might contain several different kinship groups each living in a distinct area of that town, farming, working at crafts, or carrying on local trade. The groups functioned in specific relationships to each other and to the superior authority of the locale, be it a dominant tribe, a local chief or a resident official of some still higher authority. In addition to the elements characteristic of the town, African cities included, like European cities, a rich native merchant class, numerous native political officials and religious leaders and, if it were a capital, a royal family and its court. Unlike most European cities, African cities usually had a considerable population of resident foreigners, usually a colony of Moslem traders with their families, and religious leaders.

Cities and Towns in Medieval Europe

Major features of Europe's history are the antiquity of her cities and, with the exception of the early Middle Ages, the prominence of their role in her history. Almost all of the cities and towns of Western Europe were founded in Roman or Medieval times. The major exceptions are those established as a result of state planning in the sixteenth and seventeenth centuries—capitals, fortress towns and naval bases—and recent foundations that resulted from city planning and suburban growth. Most Roman towns grew up around military camps that were strategically located. Roman military camps, in the heyday of the Empire, were essentially supply posts rather than fortresses and hence were built on sites chosen for their accessibility rather than for their defensibility. They were usually located at crossroads or river crossings instead of on remote and hard-to-reach hilltops or mountainsides. They thus became commercial centers and were insured a degree of survival. Sites for pre-Roman military foundations, Celtic fortresses for instance, were chosen for defensive purposes, and as a result relatively few of them developed into towns.

Roman urban and commercial development, at its high point in the first and second centuries, leveled off during the third century, and afterwards steadily declined. A generally reduced level of prosperity, Germanic raids, and heavy taxation in the late Imperial centuries hurt the Roman middle classes and spelled the ruin of the cities. As Roman roads and bridges (the chief avenues of trade) fell into disrepair and remained undefended, travel became increasingly subject to banditry, and commerce steadily declined. By the tenth century there were few if any cities or towns, in the economic sense, left in Western Europe. People still occupied buildings on the sites of old cities, and some congregated in new communities that grew up around castles, monasteries and cathedrals, but there were few merchants and artisans among them; most of the inhabitants worked in nearby fields for their livings.

With the population explosion and the general revival of European commercial life after 1000, however, cities and towns again came into their own. Old Roman towns, virtually abandoned for centuries, profited from their accessible locations and flourished again. On the other hand, many towns that had grown up around Medieval castles, churches and monasteries faced problems. Medieval lay and ecclesiastical lords had often chosen sites, like the earlier Celts, for defensibility— on spurs, hilltops, amid meandering courses of streams, and on islands in the middle of rivers. Some such sites were suited to the needs of the new commercial age, but many were not. Towns on navigable rivers or on islands where hard ground provided crossing places, for example, found that they could easily attract merchants, and they prospered. Those on remote and inaccessible sites could not attract traders, and as a result most frequently failed to develop.

Inhabitants of cities and towns were at first dependent for protection upon the castle, cathedral or abbey around which they were clustered. This meant that the townsmen were subject to the local ecclesiastical or lay lord. Indeed, feudal lords often founded towns on their lands in expectation of profit from them. As towns grew in number and in strength, however, townsmen developed aspirations of independence, and friction developed between them and their lords. Much of the history of the High Middle Ages is told in terms of struggle between towns and nobles. In time, however, most cities and towns won rights of self-government, sometimes peacefully by purchase of a charter, but often only at the price of open rebellion.

Medieval cities were small by modern standards; even the largest rarely approached 100,000. Milan and Venice probably reached that figure in the thirteenth century while Naples and Florence, Italy's other large cities, probably had 60,000 or 70,000. Bruges, Brussels, Louvaine, and Ypres, at the other end of the main axis of urban growth stretching from Italy to the Netherlands, had 20,000 to 40,000. Ghent, the largest city in the Netherlands, had around 56,000. The Spanish cities, Barcelona, Cordoba, Seville and Granada each had perhaps 35,000 people living in them. Paris with about 80,000, London with about 35,000, and Cologne with nearly 40,000 were the only other large cities in western and central Europe. Most towns had less than 10,000 people and the normal size was perhaps 1,000 to 3,000.

Though only a small portion of Medieval Europe's population lived in urban settlements, the towns and cities nourished many values that were to become more characteristic of the modern western civilization than did the Medieval countryside. Urban centers, often conducting their own affairs independently of the feudal system that hobbled the agrarian population were especially concerned with such things as the protection and encouragement of trade and industry, equitable and rapid business law, local government, a sound and dependable financial system, and the accumulation of wealth in goods and money rather than in land. Cities and towns remained throughout the period agricultural markets serving the needs of the countryside around them, but their greatest importance was as centers of European trade.

Europe's Commerce

For a long time after the end of the Roman empire, ancient patterns of Mediterranean trade continued, though its volume was greatly reduced. Europe continued to buy grain, oil and papyrus from North Africa, and dates, spices, silks and leather from Egyptian, Syrian and Greek merchants who had imported such goods from the East. In return Europe exported timber, metals, textiles and pottery. Gradually, however, the western Mediterranean, which had already slipped into decline in late Roman times, lagged farther and farther behind the eastern Mediterranean. By the eighth century, western and much of central Europe was an economic backwater. Mediterranean goods and Levantine merchants no longer penetrated inland, and ports died for lack of commerce. The decline of the west resulted from a combination of factors. Chief among them were the Byzantine Empire's policy of restricting its trade to its own ports, and the increasing predatory raids of Viking adventurers in the north and of Moslem pirates in the western Mediterranean.

The only real point of contact that western, northern and central Europe maintained with the eastern Mediterranean was Venice. An island republic, secure behind lagoons at the head of the Adriatic and free from most of the political troubles that plagued the mainland, Venice maintained commercial relations with Byzantium, the Arabs, and a large part of western and central Europe. Venice sold luxury goods such as spices, silk and precious stones procured in Byzantine and Arab ports to merchants in northern Italy. These merchants in turn transported them up the Po and overland through the central Alpine passes into the Rhine valley, a route that remained for centuries one of the most important in European trade. To the Arabs Venice sold arms, metals, timber and east-European slaves.

After around 1000 the sluggish economy of Europe quickened. Of the several factors that favored the revival of trade, population increase was probably basic. With the cessation of invasions, the decline of feudal anarchy, and the renewal in many places of agricultural colonization, population and production began again to grow over the whole of northwestern Europe. At the same time, a successful counteroffensive against Islam in Spain, in Sicily and in the eastern Mediterranean contributed significantly to economic revitalization. Moslem pirates were driven from the sea; European—especially Italian—merchants established commercial contacts directly with the Levant; shipbuilding grew in the west; and Crusaders began to bring home new tastes for eastern goods.

Revival of trade in the western Mediterranean was the most immediate result of the general economic recovery of Europe. The reopening of the western Mediterranean to trade meant that Europe, which, after the collapse of the Roman world, had been able to make only the slenderest contacts with the Mediterranean centers of civilization, was now brought again into direct and close touch with them. Italian cities, principally Pisa and Genoa, led the commercial revival in the western Mediterranean. Pisa, an inland river port that lay on one of the major pilgrim routes to Rome, was in a position to profit both from sea trade in luxury goods and from land trade in cheaper commodities such as grain, salt and metals. Early in the eleventh century she secured dominant positions in Corsica, Elba and Sardinia, and began commerce with southern Italy and the Balearic Islands, Spain and North Africa, trading alike with western Christians, Byzantine merchants and Arabs. Soon Genoa, which had declined almost to the point of disappearance since Roman times, was competing with Pisa. Both cities enjoyed a remarkable prosperity during the eleventh, twelfth and most of the thirteenth centuries. Both, for example, were chief ports from which crusading expeditions sailed and, as a consequence, shared in the great commercial advantages and profits that accrued from those ventures. Though her recovery began somewhat later than Pisa's, Genoa had the advantage of a more favorable location in relation to trans-Alpine European markets, and eventually completely eclipsed Pisa. Genoa acquired an especially important position in North Africa, and toward the end of the thirteenth century began experimenting in sailing directly to France, the Netherlands and England, rather than relying upon overland shipping. Meanwhile, Venice retained and even increased her commercial dominance in the eastern Mediterranean. As a result of the crusades she was able to secure control of Crete, several important harbors in Greece, the right to trade in any port of the Byzantine Empire, and a virtual monopoly on trade in the Black Sea. At the same time that trade was being revived in the western Mediterranean and expanded in the eastern Mediterranean, the North Sea and the Baltic were also experiencing an increased volume of commercial activity.

As important as the revived and expanded seaborne trade was, however, the most significant segment of Europe's commercial economy during the period between 1000 and 1300 remained overland trade. Goods transported across the Mediterranean, the North Sea or the Baltic were deposited at Europe's port cities. But that was not their final destination. Most of them were trans-shipped overland to the interior where the bulk of Europe's population lived. Commercial activity on the seas was thus but a preliminary step in Europe's trade. The seas, particularly the North Sea and the Baltic, were little more than lakes across which goods were carried in order to get them to points from which they could be carried inland to the major markets.

Four main trans-European trade routes developed: from the Baltic to the Black Sea by way of the Dvina and the Dnieper river systems that almost connect them; second, from the Baltic through the Elbe and eastern Alpine passes to the Adriatic; third, from the North sea (and England) through the Rhine and central Alpine passes to Po River basin in northern Italy; and fourth, from the English Channel through the Seine and the Rhone (or from the North Sea through the Meuse and the Rhone) to the Mediterranean. Each connected the Mediterranean to the marginal inland seas of northwestern Europe. The major commercial axis of western and central Europe thus ran from the Low Countries to northern Italy, connecting the Mediterranean ports with the ports on the northern seas. Interestingly, this is also the industrial axis of modern Europe.

The major points of contact between the merchants who brought goods from the south and those from the north were the commercial fairs held in the county of Champagne, which spanned the trade routes comprising the north-south commercial axis. These six fairs, which formed the main focus of Europe's commercial economy until the end of the thirteenth century, were held at four nearby towns in Champagne—Troyes, Provins, Bar-sur-Aube, and Lagny, all near Paris. The bulk of the commerce of the fairs was handled by caravans of pack animals that traveled the overland routes on regular schedules, though some came at least partially by way of river and lake transport. Most areas of central and western Europe—France, Italy, the Low Countries, Germany, England, Spain, Switzerland and Savoy—sent their local merchandise to the fairs along with imported goods from the Levant and Africa. All manner of goods came: cloth, wool, leather, silk, spices, furs, linen, wax, sugar, alum, lacquer, dyestuffs, cotton, as well as grain, wine and horses. The luxury goods and spices formed an especially important part of the exchange, though cloth and wool made up its greatest volume. Indeed, through the Champagne fairs flowed virtually all the cloth trade of Europe.

The Champagne fairs remained the focus of European commerce until around 1300. They declined in importance after that date for a number of related reasons. For one thing, the county of Champagne, which had been practically independent, was absorbed in 1285 into the kingdom of France and became burdened with heavier taxes and a war with Flanders, formerly one of the chief suppliers of all-important wool cloth to the Champagne markets. At the same time, more easterly overland routes into south Germany and all-sea routes through the Strait of Gibraltar and up the coast of Europe to northern ports began seriously diverting Mediterranean products that had once gone to Champagne. More important, however, was that after 1300 the whole of Europe suffered a population decline and general economic crisis that adversely affected virtually all industries and markets.

Late Medieval Crisis

Between the eleventh and the thirteenth centuries a far larger area of land than had ever been in use before, including much land of low quality that the increased use of iron implements made profitable, was brought under cultivation. But, increasingly, new lands tended to remain in the hands of single tenants rather than become part of villas. And villas themselves tended to decline in importance as their preserves fragmented. Loss of parts of large estates through illegal usurpations by tenants or estate officials, together with legal enforcement, divisions among heirs, and sale to prosperous bourgeoisie and had been going on for some time, but the pace was accelerated after the eleventh century. Thus the old-style villas were replaced by somewhat smaller, more fragmented agricultural structures frequently spoken of as manors. At the same time, service obligations of tenants, often the principal dues owed by tenants to the lord of a villa, were gradually reduced to insignificance, depriving the owner class of a valuable source of free labor as well as an important means of controlling the local economy. Tenants henceforth had greater freedom in disposing of their produce, and lords were forced to try to hire enough labor to continue to run what remained of their estates. But labor was in short supply, its cost high, and the lords' capital resources meager.

Agriculture throughout most of the Middle Ages had been dominated by grain crops—wheat, rye, spelt, oats, barley and later, buckwheat—any cereal from which bread, the mainstay of Medieval man's diet, could be made. Conditions of life were so uncertain and trade so restricted that each local community had to grow its own grain. Thus all sorts of lands were given over to its cultivation, including even rugged Alpine slopes and waterlogged lowlands. Peas and beans, grapes, fruits and a few vegetables supplemented the meager diet. But towards the end of the High Middle Ages the development of cheap water transport made possible the importation of grain from eastern Europe in huge quantities. The result was to depress grain prices in the West, cutting still further into the margin of landlords' profits and aggravating their economic misery.

One possible solution lay in the revival or expansion of slavery, at least in Italy, on some of the Mediterranean islands, and on the Iberian peninsula, where remnants of the institution had been in continual existence since the days of the Roman Empire. With the expansion of commerce in the thirteenth century, Genoese and Venetian merchants, leagued in joint-stock companies, had already established bases on the coasts of the Black Sea to purchase slaves from local Tartar and Russian princes. The slave merchants transported Tartars, Armenians, Georgians, Bulgars and Circassians to western Mediterranean markets. A slave trade with many of the appurtenances that would characterize the later Atlantic trade in human chattel quickly developed.

So did the outlines of a plantation slave economy. By 1300 there was a large-scale sugar-cane industry on the Mediterranean islands, notably Cyprus, employing slave labor on plantations that were virtually proto-types of later American creations. The European experiment with re-vived or expanded slavery reached its peak in the fourteenth and fif-teenth centuries, but quickly leveled off and, in most areas, declined when the Turks in 1453 captured Constantinople and sealed off the Black Sea ports. Afterwards, the exorbitant price for slaves in most of the West made them luxury items used mainly to decorate the courts of great princes and prelates.

On the Iberian peninsula, however, slavery continued to expand. The slave population there was already considerably larger than in the rest of the Mediterranean and, by the time the Turks ended the eastern trade, the Portuguese were establishing slaving stations on the coasts of West Africa. These new African sources continued to furnish black slaves to Portugal and Spain and would shortly supply the whole of the Americas.

Thus by around 1300 a European crisis was at hand. An expanding population had ploughed up meadows and cut down forests to make room for fields. Without pastures and woods, livestock died off and manure fell into short supply, and without grass and trees to bind the soil in place the rains caused serious erosion. Crop failures became common and widespread famine resulted. To the ecological crisis was added economic difficulty as credit facilities became saturated and commerical enterprises began to fail. Moreover, a series of epidemics, of which the mid-fourteenth century Black Death was the most famous, severely reduced populations and worsened the diseases of the econ-omy. Depression, social dislocation and political disintegration followed in swift succession.

For a hundred and fifty years, from about 1300 to about 1450, Europe was in the throes of chaos. Faced with chronic labor shortages, landlords were forced to begin breaking up their lands into smaller parcels and letting them to independent farmers on leases for specified terms of years in return for either a share of the harvest or a fixed rent instead of the older perpetual tenures. Thus lands became further fragmented and, because of the fixed-term leases, subject to relatively rapid fluctuations in management and cultivation. The landlords suffered as the returns from their holdings, which were fast becoming merely rent-paying institutions, declined relative to their expenses. Some tenants though they profited temporarily from their new freedom, were soon attracted or forced to move into growing towns and cities. The end of the crisis, which we shall examine later, came only with the general economic recovery of Europe and the development of capitalism on the eve of the opening of the Atlantic. Long before that time, however, Europe was already looking to the outside for an answer to its problems.

Europe and Africa

During the greater part of the Middle Ages Christian Europe, with its commercial interests turned inward, had slight interest and less knowledge concerning black Africa. Europe's isolation was accentuated by the conquest of North Africa by the Moslem Arabs, for they effected a political, cultural and economic barrier separating Europe from the black areas of Africa more impenetrable than the geographical barrier earlier posed by the Sahara. Moreover, almost constant struggles between Arabs and Berbers in North Africa reduced that area to an economic waste, and maritime trade in the Mediterranean in the seventh and eighth centuries came almost to a standstill.

Europeans had, from Roman times, been at least vaguely aware of black peoples. As far back as the late second and early third centuries, Christian tradition had accorded one of the Three Wise Men of the Nativity story the attributes of a black king from Sheba. Similarly, Biblical references to "Ethiopians," usually said to symbolize the remotest and most pagan of creatures and occasionally made to stand for the very antithesis of Christianity, were frequently repeated in early Christian literature and Medieval folklore. But beyond that, Europeans knew and cared little about anything beyond their own shores.

The first hints of a more serious European interest in Africa occurred during the reign of Charlemagne, around 800, who established diplomatic relations with some of the Moslem rulers in the East and in Africa. At the same time a trickle of trade between Europe and Africa reappeared as Moslems living in the desert areas found they needed

European grain and timber. By the tenth century prosperity had returned to North Africa, and Moslem merchants of the Barbary coast had become middlemen trading with galleys from Naples, Venice, Genoa, Pisa, Marseilles, on the one hand and with black Africans in the Sudan on the other. The bitterness that developed between Europeans and Moslems as a result of the Crusades in Spain and in the eastern Mediterranean did not affect Europe's commercial relationships with such North African Moslem ports as Tunis and Tripoli on the Barbary Coast. These areas maintained their independence and manifested no interest in the political affairs of their co-religionists in Spain or Syria. It is significant that, when the popes of the period pronounced their anathema against Moslems in general, they conspicuously exempted those of the Barbary coast.

Though the Barbary trade familiarized European merchants with much of the North African coast and its towns, what lay beyond, in the interior of the continent, remained a mystery to all but a few. Medieval Europe's failure to penetrate Africa contrasts sharply with the success it had in making contact with the remotest parts of Asia—witness the famous journeys to China by Marco Polo and his family. This failure must be attributed largely to the diligence of the Moslem middlemen who controlled the trans-Saharan trade. They jealously guarded their sources of supply against intrusions from European competitors.

What little knowledge of black Africa did reach Europe during these centuries came from the reports of a few merchants and missionaries who managed some travel into the interior at widely dispersed intervals. Maps made by Jewish merchants who knew the region also helped somewhat. But all such reports were fragmentary and reached only a limited audience at best. In the early twelve hundreds, for example, certain Venetian merchants seem to have traveled through the lands of the sultan of Tunis, but we have no account of what they reported. However, a few products from the southern fringes of Morocco, such as dates and alum, found their way to a few European markets where they were exchanged for cloth and leather.

The church probably never lost all touch with Christian communities in North Africa, and some early popes exchanged occasional diplomatic letters with various North African sovereigns. But these minimal formal contacts brought practically no information to Europeans about Africa. In the early thirteenth century the papacy sought, with only limited success, to secure guarantees of protection for Christians living in the domains of the sultan of Morocco. But around 1250 one European, unknown by name, traveled across the Sahara with a salt caravan to some country, possibly ancient Ghana, where, he reported, the people worshipped a dragon that lived on an island in a lake—possibly an alligator totem that the traveler mistook for a god. And a bit later, in the early fourteenth century, an Italian map-maker spoke of getting some information on the African interior from a Genoese merchant who was living in extreme southern Morocco, "near the lands of the blacks," and conducting trade by camel caravan. During the same decades the papacy sent feeble and uncertain missions up the Nile in search of rumored lost Christian communities. They, or their successors, were successful, for by the 1440's the papacy had established contact with Ethiopian Christian leaders and shortly afterwards began receiving their delegations in Rome. These church liaisons emboldened other souls to venture into the interior of Africa, including at least one Renaissance artist, a Venetian painter by the name of Niccolo Brancaleone who lived and worked in Ethiopia.

Links Through the Jews

Medieval Jews proved an especially valuable source of information on the African interior. Jews had formed an important part of the population of North Africa since very early times. Some Jews possibly came to North Africa with the Phoenicians as early as 1000 B.C., and in the sixth century B.C. a great wave of immigration brought a large Jewish population into the area. The community grew and prospered until 115 A.D. when it revolted against Roman rule. Following suppression of the revolt, many Jews fled westward and southward into the oasis of the Sahara, where their descendants remained throughout the Middle Ages. It seems likely that some Jews eventually found their way across the Sahara to the Sudan itself. In the middle of the fifteenth century a Genoese merchant, Antonio Malfante, traveling in the Sahara noted seeing numerous Jews, and an early sixteenth-century traveler, Valentin Fernandes, reported the presence in the Sudan of Jewish merchants, goldsmiths and jewelers in great numbers.

Information about the African interior filtered back, over the centuries, through the Jewish communities to a colony of Jewish cartographers on the island of Majorca. The maps that these Jews produced in the early fourteenth century were crude and inaccurate, but they served nonetheless to provide Europeans with at least some information on black Africa. For example they showed, however inexactly, the locations of such places as Timbuktu, Gao, and Mali, hitherto only names that Europeans associated vaguely with remote and rich regions. These maps set men thinking about the possibilities of reaching these places directly.

In the meantime Europe's trade in African products via the Moslem middlemen had mounted steadily. By the twelfth century many European cities had entered into formal commercial treaties with North African rulers guaranteeing the personal safety of nationals. Trading rights were established, and also sometimes resident agents and official consuls in port cities. In short, the African trade was rapidly becoming regularized. The chief difficulty that remained was the danger of piracy. Always popular with the maritime peoples of southern Europe as well as those of North Africa, piracy became a well organized and highly profitable business sometimes resorted to by otherwise respectable merchants and occasionally by entire city-states. But as troublesome as it was, piracy could not seriously retard the expanding trade. The sheer volume was too great.

By the thirteenth century Europe was sending to North Africa a varied selection of goods, many of which were trans-shipped across the Sahara to the Sudan. European copper was especially in demand in black Africa as were glass beads, most of which were made in Venice. European cloth also found an enormous market beyond the Sahara. Wine from France, Spain, and Greece flowed freely on the Barbary coast, and the shipyards of Venice and Genoa regularly built for Arab buyers. In exchange, Europe received a wide range of African goods. Despite prohibitions to the contrary, slaves, both white and black, were poured into Christian Europe by dealers in Pisa and Genoa. The coarse pepper called Grani or Paradise, from which later derived the name of the Grain Coast of West Africa, became as popular in southern France as dyed Sudan leather did in England and Normandy. Europe also offered a ready market for African ivory, ebony, and especially gold.

CHAPTER FOUR

Europe, Africa
and the Atlantic

Thus far we have followed the histories of Africa and
Europe—that is, of those areas of the two continents
lying beyond the Mediterranean orbit—to roughly the
fifteenth century. In relative isolation, Africans and
Europeans developed indigenous cultures to which they
added important elements from the civilizations of the
ancient Mediterranean. As a result, both continents
evolved separate traditions which, though they differed
greatly, were in several respects comparable. The most
densely settled areas of both continents were the large
stretches of open plains; forests, swamps, and jungles
were little used during the period we have considered.
Moreover, on both continents considerable populations
came to be concentrated in towns and cities where agricultural produce was exchanged for trade goods and

manufactured items. The urban center in turn became the focus of economic wealth and political power. And between the tenth and fifteenth centuries, both continents saw the rise and decline of several important kingdoms and empires, located for the most part in their interior reaches. Indeed, the historical development of both Africa and Europe took place largely in their interiors, along overland trade routes or in river valleys radiating from the Mediterranean and Black Seas. The great ocean that lay to the west played little part in the early histories of either continent.

The most significant development for both Europe and Africa at the end of the fifteenth and the beginning of the sixteenth centuries was the opening of the Atlantic to trade. That event forced a shift of focus from the Mediterranean westward to the Ocean Sea—an economic shift accompanied by a political shift. The areas of Europe and Africa that had grown rich, and consequently powerful, on the Mediterranean trade (the Italian and German city-states and principalities and the old Empires of the Sudan) suffered economic and political decline. In contrast, states on the Atlantic (Spain, Portugal, France, the Netherlands and England, and the new kingdoms of western and central Africa) made startling advances. They became the new powers of Europe and Africa and, eventually, partners in the colonization and exploitation of the New World.

European Recovery and Renaissance

At the opening of the fifteenth century Europe was still suffering the depopulation, depression, social dislocation and political disintegration that had blighted it since shortly after 1300. But during the latter half of the century the whole continent, particularly its Atlantic coastal states, experienced an extraordinary recovery. By the end of the century Europeans had not only restored political order, social stability and economic prosperity, they had also taken impressive strides in scholarship, arts and letters, and had launched a spectacular series of world explorations and found a New World. These accomplishments were so rapid and so impressive that many historians have viewed them as marking a kind of rebirth of European civilization—a Renaissance.

Fundamental to European recovery was population growth that had been checked and eventually reversed by incessant wars, plagues, and famines since 1300. Around the middle of the fifteenth century, however, as peace was restored and plagues abated, population burgeoned. By 1500 it was at 70,000,000, an increase of around forty percent above what it was around 1400. The economy responded. Increased demand drove prices up and encouraged improvements in technology, communication and transportation, as well as innovations in business practices.

Feudal nobles, the dominant class in the Middle Ages, declined in both wealth and importance, while the long-suffering serfs improved their lot dramatically. Aristocratic landlords found themselves forced to sell their produce—mostly grain and wine—for less and less because of overproduction resulting from improved agricultural techniques and competition from imports from eastern Europe. At the same time they had to pay higher wages to their workers. Conversely, the serfs, whose labor was in demand on both manors and in towns, commanded high enough pay to free themselves from old medieval restrictions and begin either to lease their own land or go to work in industry.

Changes in Land Use and Ownership

The pressures and problems of the fourteenth and fifteenth centuries brought dark days, but the foundation of western Europe's economy— the manorial system—survived albeit substantially altered. Different areas generated different adaptations to the crisis. In eastern Europe, circumstances favored revivification and expansion of the traditional system. There landlords, growing grain for sale in the rapidly expanding western European market, pressed into service every acre of land and every able hand. Direct exploitation of tenants, extension of the demesne, increases in the labor services required of servile tenants, and augmented authority of landlords were the results. In the west, on the other hand, estate organization and the relationship of landlord and tenant changed greatly. To forestall desertion by their tenants, who were being enticed by the new urban economies, landlords frequently altered traditional contracts and granted new freedoms, modifying duration, price and details of land leases. Some even rented out parts of their huge holdings, retaining direct control only of what they could profitably exploit.

Such changes in the patterns of estate management undermined the traditional personal basis of European agriculture. Landowners thenceforth often lived in town and rarely saw their tenants, dealing with them only through agents. In areas where the ancient institution of slavery had survived, particularly Spain, Italy, and the Mediterranean islands, it was expanded in an attempt to make farming pay. Everywhere lands were more frequently sold than formerly, and owners came increasingly to view their holdings less as family patrimonies to be handed on to sons and grandsons, and more as business operations to be held only as long as they were profitable. Their tenants were no longer personal wards, so to speak, but merely names in account books. Strictly legal contracts governing lands and labor replaced interpersonal bonds, as profit and loss transformed the traditional way of life.

The new type of landlord reorganized their estates with an eye towards efficiency. A few prosperous old landowners, who were able to hold on and adjust to the new conditions, and many new capitalist investors, grown rich on the commercial revolution already well under way in the west, began to buy up lands and convert them into new and more profitable uses. The new owners were determined to extract as much profit as possible. Marginal land that had been pressed into service during the great age of clearing was allowed to return to scrub, heath, forest or marsh, and tillage of fertile areas was rearranged so that they could be worked more intensively than ever. With the importation of cheap grain from eastern Europe, cereal production in the west was increasingly abandoned, and individual regions began to specialize in producing commodities for which they were particularly suited. The Low Countries produced dairy products, southern Germany and certain areas in France gave over large tracts to wine grapes, and other areas specialized in fruit crops. Old grain crops were replaced by leguminous plants and industrial products such as cole seed for oil; madder, woad, and weld for dyes; hops; mulberry trees for silkworms to feed on; flax and pasture.

Sheep farming was typical of the new uses to which land was being put by the new owners: it was large-scale with capitalist organization; its major product, wool, was intended for a large industrial market; it made profitable use of land unprofitable under cultivation; and its sole object was to draw maximum profit from its operation. Thus, the framework of the manor, a regenerated and invigorated capitalist owner class, a respect for the law of contract, and awareness of new techniques, and new conceptions of estate organization and management characterized the agriculture of Renaissance Europe. Once the Atlantic was opened, these concepts would be carried over to the Americas.

The Rise of Businessmen

The primary beneficiaries of the economic and social upheavals were the urban merchants. Because of rising prices and increasing demand, they stood to make a profit on virtually anything they bought and resold. Traders opened new overland and sea routes, merchants formed joint-stock companies, financiers undertook deposit banking, insurance guarantees and credit expansion, and great capitalists underwrote the establishment of huge banking and commercial enterprises extending all across Europe. Businessmen in general employed new and more efficient systems of accounting and business management, maintaining, for example, offices where they studied and analyzed reports and accounts instead of trusting to intuition and chance. By the end of the century the wealth of some merchants, manufacturers and bankers was rivaling that of princes.

For their part, the princes and kings of Europe, acutely conscious of the unprecedented expansion of business, sought to turn it to their advantage. They began to finance certain industries that required outlays of capital too large for most private financiers to manage, and at the same time they worked at encouraging the establishment of new industries within their states, in early anticipation of mercantilism. One of the most important industries developed largely at state expense was mining. Always in need of precious metals for coins, lesser metals for arms, and minerals for trade, rulers all over Europe invested heavily in mines and took an active part in their management. Though the production of silver and iron quintupled in the century after 1450, it never seemed enough. And gold had long been scarce. The thirst for precious metals, particularly gold, was to be one of the chief motivating factors leading to explorations, new discoveries, and the opening of the Atlantic.

Europe, Africa and Gold

Europe never had many gold sources of her own—only a few alluvial deposits that she supplemented with imports. These had been sufficient for the Romans and some of the successor barbarian kingdoms to maintain a gold coinage but, after the decline in trade around 500 A.D., the supply of gold in Europe began to dwindle significantly. Some had been buried in times of distress and forgotten, some had been looted by invaders, some was spent for Asian luxuries. As a result of the steady drain, most western European kingdoms ceased to strike gold coins. Instead, the silver penny or denier became, for some five centuries, the characteristic coin of western Europe, though a few antique, foreign or ornamental gold pieces were occasionally seen.

With the opening of the new markets in North Africa in the thirteenth century, however, Europe began to recoup her gold reserves. She could now transport her bulky trade goods cheaply by water across the Mediterranean to Barbary ports and exchange them for Sudan gold. From the mysterious gold fields deep in black Africa—much of it from the fabled mine of Wangara—the gold was brought, usually in dust form, to the great African commercial cities on the Southern borders of the Sahara such as Timbuktu. There it was refined and sent by camel-back across the desert to the North African port cities where Europe's merchants waited with their wares. Enriched by the influx of African gold, various European kingdoms and city-states experimented with issuing new gold coins, and in 1252 Florence struck the florin. That famous coin became the prototype of the new gold issues that soon followed from one after another western European country. A few years later, in 1284, Venice issued her gold ducat that filled a similar role in eastern Mediterranean trade.

Even with the buoying effect of the gold imports from Africa, Europe's economy remained in constant need of precious metals. The supply of bullion from Africa did not keep pace with the increasing demand for money, and the development of credit often was not sufficient to balance the deflationary pressure. Around 1300 the fiscal crisis, aggravated by the series of long wars and devastating plagues, plunged Europe into a century and a half of depression and chaos. As she began to recover from this trauma around the middle of the fifteenth century, Europe found her gold reserves again dangerously depleted. Her bankers and merchants turned their eyes, as they had in the past, to Africa. But this time they were not content to trade for gold with the Moslem middlemen; the Europeans wanted to seize control of the supply center itself. About the middle of the fifteenth century the Genoese merchant Antonio Malfante set out in search of the sources of Africa's gold supply, never to return. From the central Sahara he sent back his one and only communication, saying that he had asked repeatedly, but that no one seemed to know where the gold originated, only that it came from far away. So Europe's efforts to penetrate the Sahara failed. But she was determined, and her princes, bankers, and adventurers devised a new plan—to tap Africa's gold resources via a sea route.

Opening the Atlantic

Early isolated ventures into the Atlantic, whether timorous voyages along the West African and European coasts by fifth-century B.C. Greeks and Carthaginians and Medieval Arabs, or the fascinating explorations of Greenland and Vinland by Norsemen from the tenth to the fourteenth centuries, contributed little or nothing to the opening of the Atlantic. These adventurers failed to understand what they had found and were unable to make any practical use of it. The real opening of the Ocean came only in the latter fifteenth century.

Several earlier historical developments, however, paved the way. Medieval legend and romance, including fanciful stories of Alexander the Great's conquests of fabulous Asian kingdoms and the Apostle Thomas's conversion of India to Christianity, had established in the European mind a marvelous vision of the East. The most persistent and influential Medieval myth was the cherished legend of Prester John. The Prester was said to be a Christian monarch ruling a great, rich, and powerful kingdom somewhere in Asia, or perhaps Africa. A descendant of one of the Three Wise Men who came to adore the infant Christ, Prester John was supposedly waiting in hope of reuniting his lost Christian kingdom with the rest of Christendom. Popular accounts written by travelers to the East, such as Marco Polo in the thirteenth century, further excited the Europeans' imaginations concerning Asia at the same time that spices, drugs, jewels, fine cloth and great quantities of slaves imported from Asia and the Black Sea area were whetting European appetites. As a result, Italian merchants developed a thriving trade in oriental goods and slaves that enriched them momentarily, but in the long run dangerously depleted Europe's gold reserves.

In the fourteenth and early fifteenth centuries, the Ottoman Turks conquered the lands at the eastern end of the Mediterranean and began to compete with Europeans in the Asian luxury and slave trade, forcing the Italian merchants to look for new markets for their own goods as well as cheaper sources of supply for imports. At this juncture the growing economic importance of England and the Netherlands, particularly in cloth manufacture, attracted the attention of Italian merchants, who thought this might be the answer to their quest for a new market. In an attempt to tap the newly discovered market most advantageously, they began to send trading galleys around Gibraltar and through Atlantic water to the ports of western Europe rather than use the traditional slower, more expensive overland trade routes through central Europe. As profitable as the new north European trade was, it could not provide the gold Europe sought. But the experience gained from making contact with the northern markets via sea routes proved, ultimately, of critical importance.

With increased use of the seas, better navigation aids had to be developed. Mediterranean mariners had used a primitive compass since the thirteenth century, but it was of limited value because they did not understand its magnetic variations from true north, a problem that was not solved until well into the sixteenth century. In the fifteenth century, seamen also began to use simple versions of the quadrant and the astrolabe, but again their use on board ship was limited because of the pitch and roll of the vessel. Once out of sight of land a fifteenth-century captain had to determine his position solely by dead reckoning —an estimate of the distance he had traveled along the the course he was steering, arrived at by judging the speed of this ship in relation to the time he had been sailing. Since the late thirteenth century, navigators had also used parchment portulan charts drawn to show courses, distances, and latitudes (relatively accurate for the small Mediterranean but very misleading in the large Atlantic) as well as outlines of coasts, harbors and islands. As new coasts and islands were explored, cartographers added them to their charts.

Prince Henry of Portugal

Systematic exploration and exploitation of the Atlantic was first undertaken by Portugal. A narrow coastal strip of a country with a large portion of its population already engaged in fishing and trading on the sea, Portugal was ideally suited to such an undertaking. She was also fortunate to have the services of one of the greatest figures in the history of exploration, Prince Henry the Navigator. Prince Henry was especially interested in Africa. He studied its peoples, its religions, its trade routes and its resources, particularly reports of gold mines in its interior. African gold sources had long been a key factor in Europe's economy, and Europeans now determined to find a route directly to them to avoid the Moslem middlemen from whom Europeans had thitherto been forced to purchase most of their gold supply. Prince Henry also became convinced that the ruler of Abyssinia, the exact location of which still remained a mystery to European geographers though they were sure that it was in Africa, was the fabled Prester John who, if the Christian powers could but establish contact with him, would join them in a war against the common Moslem enemy. The interest in Africa generated by the search for Prester John was augmented, moreover, by the tradition that one of the Three Wise Men was king of Sheba. By the early fifteenth century European artists, even in Germany and the Netherlands, were portraying him as a black man. Finding both a plentiful supply of gold and a powerful Christian ally in Africa thus became Prince Henry's dream.

But he was much more than a dreamer. He established a kind of center for the study and planning of African exploration and invited to it leading scientists, seamen and technicians from all over Europe. With their help he outfitted and sent out several expeditions which successfully colonized the Madeiras and the Azores, and in the 1440's pushed down the African coast to discover the mouths of the Senegal and Gambia rivers and the Cape Verde Islands. The explorers found little gold and no Christians, but they began trading eagerly with black Africans in ivory, pepper, and slaves. The taking of slaves, though incidental in volume when compared to developments two or three centuries later, was nonetheless important enough by 1448 for the Portuguese to build a slave stockade on the island of Arguin, the first such European installation in western Africa. Atlantic trade, only minor at first, would mount gradually and, following the discovery of the Americas, dramatically.

During the twenty years following the death of Prince Henry in 1460, the Portuguese crown manifested little interest in sponsoring further explorations, though private merchants involved in the African trade made a few casual explorations on their own, including discovering what came to be called the Gold Coast. When John II became king in 1481, however, he revived official interest in Africa. Like Prince Henry before him, John was interested in opening a direct route to Africa's gold mines, finding Prester John's Abyssinia, and making Christian converts, but he had a new dream too. He wanted to find a way around Africa to India. To these ends he ordered out a whole series of expeditions. The first reached the Congo River in 1482 and the last found the Cape of Good Hope and the route to India in 1488. The eastern Atlantic was open and it belonged to Portugal.

The Africa Portugal Found

In an earlier chapter we followed the developement, roughly to the fifteenth century, of several of the old empires that were strung across the interior Sudan belt of Africa—Ghana, Mali, Songhai, Kanem-Bornu and the Hausa kingdoms. These states, oriented to the Mediterranean world and heavily dependent upon trans-Saharan trade, had their historic fates sealed at the end of the fifteenth century by the opening of the Atlantic. For other areas of the continent, however, specifically the rain forests on the Atlantic coast, the doors to the future were opened. Hitherto remote from the mainstream of western civilization, these areas suddenly found themselves critically close to its new center—the Atlantic Ocean—and were quickly drawn, via the slave trade, into a rapidly developing maelstrom.

People had been living in or near the rain forests since before the beginning of the Christian era, but until relatively late they seem to have been in primitive stages of political organization, without leaders or any kind of governmental structure. But sometime around the twelfth century they began to form states, and by the time the Portuguese arrived in the fifteenth century, they had developed full-fledged kingdoms. They also had developed a sophisticated agriculture and a knowledge of iron, and they carried on trade in gold, kola nuts and ivory, materials that they exchanged for metals, cloth, beads and cowry shells—the common currency throughout much of Africa—from the empires of Ghana, Mali, Songhai and the Hausa states to the north.

Their accomplishments in agriculture were particularly impressive. We have already noted the development of agriculture in the African Sudan belt, but solving the problems of food production in the savanna country of the Sudan did not solve them for the rain-forest areas. The humid and overgrown forests of the Guinea coast, the Congo basin and the

east-central African lowlands presented formidable obstacles to cultivators. Recent archaeological finds of stone hoes, picks and axes, however, indicate that Africans early cleared some areas in the forest region
and planted crops, probably varieties of yams and "Kaffir potatoes."
The real development of agriculture in the jungle, however, came later,
after the beginning of the Christian era, when the Africans borrowed
tropical plants. From Asia bananas, sugar cane, cucumbers, ginger and
several new varieties of rice found their way into the African tropics
where native farmers adapted them to their needs, supplementing the
yams, squash, peanuts, okra, tamarind and kola nuts they already knew.
In time African farmers became skilled cultivators of various edible
tubers, cotton and tobacco. African agriculture, as it developed during
these centuries—during the same time Europe was undergoing her "dark
ages"—was, in short, equal to any in the world.

The Kingdom of Benin

One of the oldest and certainly the most famous of the Guinea coast
states was the kingdom of Benin, on the west bank of the mouth of the
Niger. Already thriving—its capital city measured three miles in length
and the kingdom itself 250 miles across—when the Portuguese arrived
on the West African shores in 1475, Benin was still strong enough in the
late nineteenth century to resist the British advances into Africa. Oral
tradition has it that the royal dynasty, which still rules today, was
established when the people of Benin sent to Ife, an inland city-state,
asking that a royal prince come to rule them. Modern studies comparing
the political institutions of Benin with those of the Ife region generally
support some such probability. We also know from Portuguese accounts
that, in the fifteenth century, the kings of Benin were formally invested
with their authority by the kings of Ife. From British accounts in the
nineteenth century we learn that at that time the kings of Benin still
recognized the overlordship of Ife and had their bodies sent there for
ceremonial burial in a special cemetery set aside for them.

Indeed, from the beginning, the monarchs at Benin surrounded themselves with an especially high degree of ritual and ceremony implying
their supernatural powers. One of the early kings introduced a whole
galaxy of new gods whose worship involved the special royal powers
over nature. The impressive works of art resulting from brass casting,

already described as closely associated with royal lineage and religion, was a particularly important means of edifying the populace and impressing upon them the spiritual authority of their kings. In time, particularly after the seventeenth century, the kings became almost exclusively occupied with ritual observances, giving up entirely their earlier role as military leaders. Living in seclusion in their vast palaces they became the centers of an enormously complex ceremonial in which human sacrifice and cannibalism were important elements. The mysteries of the secluded priest-king and his human sacrifices made Benin the symbol of everything the western world's popular imagination associated with the jungles of Africa.

Human sacrifice was practiced in a number of areas of western and central Africa, but by no means in all. The primary object of the rite was essentially the same as it was in the societies of Greece, Rome, early Europe, and South and Central America—that of offering a single chosen human life to the controlling forces of nature as a substitute for the many victims that nature was constantly threatening to claim through famine and pestilence. In Benin, if too much rain, too hot a sun, too long a drought, or a disease of epidemic proportions endangered the community, the people expected their especially empowered king to propitiate the menace by a sacrifice. The victim—frequently female—was chosen from among alien slaves, criminals, or the badly diseased; a message to the sun god was put in her mouth; she was clubbed to death; and her body displayed for a period on a scaffold at the top of a tree. In some cases the body was later recovered and consumed by the priests or the people in ceremonial cannibalism. In another case reported by an observer, too much rain threatened the crops and the king had all his jewels brought out and placed in a heap on the ground. The chosen victim was compelled to kneel over them and the king pierced the skin of his head and neck with a spear so that blood ran down over the ornaments. The victim was instructed to tell the rain god that thenceforth when the king wore these jewels, he would have the power to keep away bad things. The victim was then led out and beheaded, and his body displayed for a time and eventually eaten. In later times human substitute-messenger victims came to be replaced by bullocks especially reserved and fattened for the purpose.

The state that the kings of Benin ruled evolved a high level of political organization. At first the new dynasty seems to have had little actual authority; instead they simply presided over the kingdom while the real power remained in the hands of local chiefs. Fairly soon, however, one of the kings—tradition says the fourth of the line—overcame this obstacle to the exercise of royal power by creating a bureaucracy of advisers, palace administrators and military commanders. When his new personal bureaucracy was sufficiently strong to counterbalance the power of the local chiefs, the king forced the latter to organize themselves into a single association which he, with the aid and support of his bureaucratic staff, dominated and directed. In time, some seven reigns later says tradition, the palace staff themselves began to threaten royal authority, and the crown had to find a way of limiting their power. This was accomplished by creating a new order of titled officials, appointed at the king's pleasure, usually from commercial classes rather than traditional leadership groups, and handing over to them such important functions as command of the armies. The new association of title holders balanced the powerful court officials and preserved final authority for the king. Over the centuries, several new orders of titled officials were added, usually from new power groups that had arisen in the community and always with the aim of protecting and promoting royal prerogative—a process not unlike the accommodation of the bourgeoisie occurring at the same time in Europe. The result was a great, largely non-hereditary hierarchy, open to able men from all over the kingdom, which could be counted upon to further the interests of the crown.

Benin's Expanding Influence

Effective centralized and largely autocratic royal government enabled the Edo people of the small forest kingdom of Benin to impose their rule on one nearby people after another and create, in time, one of the most powerful, if small—it was barely larger than the Netherlands—states of West Africa. One of the chief motives for expansion was economic. Benin was accustomed to trade and, like most of the new states that were to develop on the Guinea coast, had a well developed system of both currency—in the form of cowry shells—and weights and measure. The cowry-shell currency, used for buying and selling and at least partial satisfaction of tax levies and payment of fines, allowed the accumulation of liquid wealth that could be mobilized expeditiously and manipulated easily. With such a money economy at their disposal,

Benin and the other new coastal kingdoms of West Africa were able to develop sophisticated economic specializations, for they could easily dispose of surpluses through sale. The wealth thus generated, in turn, financed expanded economic and political ambitions of the ruling classes.

Some communities seem to have submitted to the Edo voluntarily while others were simply conquered, but all were held in awe by the magical and military might of the divine ruler. Many of the subject peoples, especially those with little in the way of indigenous political institutions, adopted those of their Benin masters, thus producing the appearance of administrative uniformity throughout much of the domain. In reality, however, the kingdom remained heterogeneous, held together only by the prestige and power of the strong kingship. Even so, the state's structure proved viable and stable enough to insure the survival of the kingdom for some five hundred years. It was not until 1897 that its kings were driven out and its territories amalgamated into Great Britain's African colonial empire.

The Kingdom of Oyo

Northwest of the forested coastal kingdom of Benin and slightly inland arose the kingdom of Oyo, half in the lower savanna and half in the forests. Oyo was one of several small principalities created by Yoruba peoples, who, like the people of Benin, traced their political origins to Ife. Their political consolidations, however, seem to have taken place somewhat later than those of Benin. Favored by its strategic location astride the trade routes from the southern forests to the markets of the western Sudan, and by its open terrain (which facilitated communications as well as horse breeding), Oyo began to extend its influence over neighboring Yoruba states. Spearheaded by their famous cavalry, Oyo's armies pushed north to the Niger river, northeast and south as far as the hill country and the forests, neither of which their horses could negotiate, and southeast until stopped by the powerful Edo of the kingdom of Benin. Oyo thus established itself in the fourteenth and fifteenth centuries as an inland power still looking northward for what contact it had with the outside world.

The Oyo kingdom was, like most West African and Sudan states, a monarchy, ruled by a divine king who lived in seclusion in his palace and devoted much of his time to carefully ordered ritual and ceremony.

But it was not an absolute monarchy; the king, called the Alafin, was subject to a series of checks and balances built into the traditional constitution of the kingdom. First of all, the crown was never inherited by the eldest son of the ruling Alafin because that prince was forced to commit suicide by drinking poison immediately following the death of his father—a precaution against overweening father-son combinations. A new king was chosen by a council of seven chiefs from among candidates put forth by the several branches of the royal lineage. Once enthroned, the king ruled with the advice of—and in certain cases, such as the declaring of war, only with the consent of—the council, whose head acted as a sort of prime minister of the realm. In extreme cases the council could reject the king completely and force him to commit suicide so that they could choose a more competent or compatible successor. In turn the council itself was subject to the Ogboni Society, an association composed of important political, commercial and religious leaders and representing the whole kingdom. This large order mediated between the king and the council when they were in conflict and held a kind of final ratification or veto power. In such a system particularly able and resolute Alafins could, and often did, by resourceful manipulation and show of force, have their way; but with weaker personalities on the throne, all the constitutional restraints came into play protecting local rights and powers.

The kings ruled the city of old Oyo and the area immediately surrounding it through their palace officials and chief priests, generally keeping that area of the realm in firm control. Their authority in the remainder of the kingdom, however, was considerably less complete. There their rule was by and large indirect, and provincial towns and subject states retained a large measure of independence. The extent of the royal authority in the outlying areas was often little more than the presence of a crown agent stationed in a locality to observe and report on administration rather than to supervise or direct it—a stage of development roughly analagous to western European monarchies such as France in say, the sixteenth century. The chief functional importance of such local royal agents was the collection of tribute due the Alafin. Thus the kings of Oyo presided, unlike those of Benin, with only severely limited powers over a largely decentralized, if extensive, state, and had to rely more on personal ingenuity than on political institutions for the effective exercise of crown power.

Taking advantage first of the Sudan trade and later of that of the

Atlantic coast, Oyo became a rich and powerful commercial state with nearly all the peoples living in towns or cities. Its capital at Old Oyo, the deserted ruins of which are visible even today beneath thick over-growth in a remote northeastern corner of the Western State of modern Nigeria, was the major trading center of the region, conducting a market regularly every four days. The city, covering some fifteen to twenty square miles and enclosed with earthwork walls, supported a large population—evidenced by the abundance of artifacts still scattered about its surface. From her savanna and forest regions, Oyo sent kola nuts, pepper, cloth, low grade salt, and possibly a few slaves north in exchange for horses, sodium carbonate (used as a bleaching agent and medicine), swords, knives, leather goods, glass beads, silks and the precious cowry shells.

Development of Oyo, Coastal Trade

Not until around the end of the sixteenth century did Oyo begin to develop its coastal trade. Oral traditions of the Yoruba credit one of their kings, Obalokun by name, with starting trade with the Atlantic coasts and with it the the political expansion southward to protect it. The drive to the south and southwest was of utmost importance to Oyo for it brought it closer to the seashores where Europeans had already established trading posts. From the European merchants on the coast the Yorubas began to get iron tools, high-grade salt, fine cloth, trinkets such as mirrors, and a variety of edged weapons—though not firearms, until the nineteenth century—in return for slaves. As a result of the new southern coastal trade, Oyo prospered and grew, reaching its zenith in the seventeenth and early eighteenth centuries when it was the largest kingdom in West Africa in terms of population and about the size of England in area.

Ironically, the same coastal trade that made Oyo rich and powerful proved a large factor in bringing the kingdom down. The economic as well as the political center of the kingdom was in its formative centuries always in its northern interior. Oyo's trade was oriented north to the Sudan rather than to the sea; its richest lands, the savanna country, lay in its northern half; its most populous and prosperous towns and cities were all in the north; even its capital was almost two hundred miles inland. The southern coastal regions were, on the other hand, sparsely populated and, as we have seen, largely independent of royal control.

The shift of the economic center of the kingdom from the northern plains to the southern coastal regions, caused by the opening of the Atlantic and the slave trade, brought new wealth and increased power for a time, but, in the end, spelled the doom of Oyo. After the economic shift southward, the constitutionally weak kings, never having had effective control of the southern area, were more than ever unable to impose their authority there. By the last quarter of the eighteenth century, the central government, weakened by a military decline and a series of bloody power struggles within the palace, had practically ceased to function. Revolts flared up, vassal states seeking more profits for themselves rebelled, particularly those near the coast, and the neighboring principalities began to dismember the Oyo domain. By the opening decades of the nineteenth century, the kingdom of Oyo had completely disintegrated, leaving in its place only a series of tiny successor states.

Central Africa

The rain forests reach down along the Guinea coast to the mouth of the Congo River and from thence inward to engulf the upper reaches of the Congo basin. South of the Congo River, however, another wide belt of savanna country with rolling plains, tall grass and fringes of woods in the river valleys stretches from the Atlantic coast across the continent to the lake district. Until the fifteenth century that part of Africa was even more isolated than the Guinea coast. The Bantu groups who had migrated into the area over the past thousand years or so had, as far as we know, no contacts with the Mediterranean and, few if any, with the east coast of Africa. Nonetheless, they developed a relatively high order of agriculture and technology, together with social and political organization. They used agricultural implements much as the hoe and the axe to cultivate millet and sorghum, and had domesticated pigs, sheep, chickens and cows. They knew how to mine, smelt and work both copper and iron, they were skilled at weaving raffia, and made decorated pottery. They had a few glass beads they might have brought with them on their earlier migrations or possibly got via long-distance trade with the east coast, and they certainly traded amongst themselves in the salt they mined. They lived in villages, and some groups buried their dead in large cemeteries, placing alongside the bodies vessels and per-

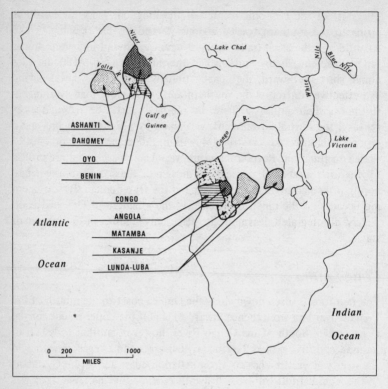

Guinea Coast Kingdoms

sonal objects such as belts, pins and ornaments. About details of their social and political organization before the fifteenth century we know almost nothing, for oral tradition does not reach that far back into their history, and archaeological work has thus far told us little. But the few sites that have been excavated indicate the existence of sizeable communities or states. We know for certain that by the time the first Europeans arrived in the late fifteenth century numerous principalities and several kingdoms existed, of which the most important were the kingdoms of Congo and Angola.

The Congo Kingdom

When the Portuguese explorers discovered the great Congo River in

1482, they also found, lying on its southern banks, the hitherto unknown kingdom of Congo. It was roughly a rectangle running 200 miles along the Atlantic coast and 250 miles inland, an area nearly half again as large as Portugal. The Congo state arose in the fourteenth century when a conquering chief who subdued an area near the center of what was later to become the kingdom, married into the local leadership lineage, established a capital at Mbanza—present-day Sao Salvador—and took the title Mani Congo or king of Congo. The new kingdom then proceeded to subdue neighboring principalities, absorbing them or forcing them into the position of tributary states.

The organization of the Congo kingdom was similar to, though more highly developed than, that of the remaining independent states of east-central Africa. At the base were villages, the headships of which were hereditary. Villages were grouped in districts headed by chiefs appointed by and serving at the pleasure of the king. They acted both as administrators and judges. The districts constituted six provinces ruled by governors, most of whom were appointed by the king, the rest holding their offices through inheritance. All were subject to removal by the crown. The king and palace councillors, in turn, supervised the governors. The king was elected from among the descendents of the founding monarch—a group so large that its members constituted a whole class unto themselves—by a council convened specifically for that purpose and composed of governors and other special officials. The king was in theory absolute, and indeed in practice exercised great power, though factional struggles during royal elections tended at times to divide the kingdom. He maintained no standing army, only a slave bodyguard, but in time of emergency ordered his territorial officials to call up warriors to form a national army.

Royal revenue derived from tribute, taxation, tolls, fees and proceeds from the crown enterprises. Once a year local officials and envoys from subject states appeared before the king and presented him with the taxes or tribute from their territories—ivory, hides, raffia cloth and slaves. Tolls and fees came likewise in kind. And royal fisheries on the coast provided *nzimbu* shells which served as currency in the kingdom. The king's riches were looked after by a group of officials who constituted a sort of treasury staff, supervising collection and expenditures. The king used his income for the maintenance of his palace staff, his court and his bodyguard, and for supplying rich gifts to influential personages of the kingdom whose favor or support he needed.

When the first Portuguese explorers landed on the Congo coast in

1482, they were immediately impressed with the friendly reception they received from the Congolese. They established relations with the king, Nzinga Kuwu, and in three years were conducting an exchange of diplomatic envoys between the Congolese and Portuguese crowns. Soon officials and students from the kingdom of Congo began to go for extended stays and study in Lisbon, and Portuguese officers, artisans and priests came to Congo to explore the region, build churches, and convert the population. In 1491 the king himself was baptised and changed his name to John I.

Links Between Congo and Portugal

The cooperation between Congo and Portugal was carried still further by the next Congolese king, Dom Affonso I (1503-43). Devoted to the Christian faith and enchanted with the idea of Europeanization, he determined to acquire for his kingdom the benefits of both. He appealed for aid to the king of Portugal who promptly sent him blacksmiths, architects, masons, schoolteachers, priests, political and military advisers, women servants to teach European household arts to the Congolese, and even printers. Under the influence of these emigrants the captial city, renamed Sao Salvador by Affonso, flourished as Portuguese artisans constructed public buildings, trade markets and churches. Teachers established schools, and priests set about converting the people. One of the king's sons, baptised Dom Henrique, after studying in Lisbon and Rome, was ordained a priest, consecrated a bishop, and returned home to work with his people.

For his part, the Portuguese king expected certain returns. He accepted the copper anklets and the few slaves sent him by Affonso as gifts, but he had greater things in mind. He wanted a monopoly on all Congo trade for Portugal, and he confidently predicted that his explorers would find a route through Congo to the fabled lost Christian kingdom of Prester John which his geographers assured him was close by. He also believed that Congo bordered the settlements that Portugal already had in Mozambique as well as rich black empires in the interior of east Africa. By aiding the development of the kingdom of Congo and maintaining friendly relations with it, Portugal could, from his point of view, only stand to gain enormously.

The extraordinary and promising experiment in foreign aid and voluntary acculturation, however, proved short-lived. The first trouble developed over the slave trade. The Portuguese residents in Congo quickly found that they could profit much more from dealing in slaves than they could from plying their trades. Most of them began to demand their wages in slaves, whom they in turn sold to traders. Many, particularly the clerics, who had become familiar with the interior reaches of the kingdom as a result of their missionary travels, undertook actual panyarring—*i.e.*, slave-catching—expeditions both within the kingdom and in borderlands. Affonso, distressed at the enslavement of his own people, if not of his neighbors, appealed in 1526 to the king of Portugal to halt the traffic, pointing out that many Congolese nobles and even members of the royal family were regularly being kidnapped. Receiving no help from Portugal, Affonso attempted to curb the practices himself, but was frustrated by the discovery that many of his own officials, especially at the local levels, were involved in the nefarious trade.

Portuguese slavers who found a ready market for their wares in the eastern Mediterranean had, only a few years before, effectively ended the importation of slaves from the Black Sea area. Europe imported around five hundred black slaves a year in the latter fifteenth and early eighteenth centuries. Spain, in particular, bought black slaves from the Portuguese for work in mining industries. Indeed, Negroes gradually replaced Arabs and east European slaves in the lowest segment of the labor force in Spain. The Portuguese and Spanish trade in black slaves would slowly shift from the Mediterranean to the islands of Portugal and West Africa, and finally across the Atlantic to the Americas.

Relations between Congo and Portugal, already strained by the slave trade, were finally broken by disputes over precious metals. The Portuguese king came to believe, mistakenly, that the kingdom of Congo controlled fabulously rich secret gold and silver mines in addition to the copper deposits that he already knew were there. When Affonso denied their existence, the Portuguese assumed that he was lying. After that point trust evaporated and relations deteriorated rapidly. Portuguese aid dropped off, Congolese interest in Europeanization declined, and friction between the two governments increased.

In the following decades illegal slave trade, corrupt missionary activities, and continuing arguments over the mines increasingly plagued the nation. Competition among rival factions of Portuguese residents for influence in Congo divided the kingdom, and struggles for the throne, lawlessness and revolts resulted. In 1568 the greatly weakened kingdom was invaded by the cannibalistic armies of the neighboring Jaga people. The Jagas destroyed Sao Salvador and wrecked the kingdom, but made no attempt to conquer and rule it; instead they moved on to ravage other areas, leaving the ruined state to linger on in near anarchy. By the end of the eighteenth century the Congo had shrunk to a tiny area around Sao Salvador; little remained of its Christianity and less of its former riches and power.

Angola

When relations with the Congo kingdom worsened after the middle of the sixteenth century, the Portuguese began to look elsewhere for an easy supply of slaves. They found it in the kingdom of Ndongo, or Angola as they called it after the title of its king, the *ngola*. Ndongo originated as a small chieftaincy on the southern border of the Congo kingdom around 1500, and grew within fifty years into a coastal kingdom about a hundred miles wide and two hundred miles deep. From the beginning its rulers actively sought to attract the Portuguese, hoping thereby to increase their prestige as well as enrich themselves. A few traders came in the 1540's and the Portuguese crown half-heartedly sent a small official mission in 1560. The leader of the mission, Paul Dias, upon arriving in Ndongo immediately perceived the potential importance of the area, and when he returned to Portugal he presented a plan to the king. Dias proposed to conquer and colonize Angola at his own expense in return for which he would be made governor and receive a huge land grant in the colony. The king agreed and in 1571 granted him his request. Dias returned to Angola four years later, established a settlement on the island of Luanda, and began conquest of the Ndongo kingdom.

The young conquistador was initially successful, but unexpected resistance from the Ndongolese and interference from European competitors dragged out the conquest for a century. In the course of these wars the Portuguese introduced a new factor in conquest and colonization. They began to train bands of local warriors in the use of firearms and send them against the Ndongolese. The first group thus used were the dreaded Jagas. The practice of arming and using African allies against recalcitrant African states became, in time, a policy common to all

European powers in Africa as well as in the rest of the world. The Portuguese steadily extended their control over Angola—except for the period between 1641 and 1648 when their Dutch enemies temporarily seized control of the area—and by the end of the seventeenth century the whole region, and along with it an enormous slave trade, was securely in their hands.

The new colony—the first substantial one in Africa, and ironically, one of the last remaining today—was organized by the Portuguese along lines that were not to change much until the twentieth century. A crown-appointed governor sat at Luanda, the capital and main port, and theoretically exercised control over the colony. In practice, however, he had to share his authority with the city council—made up at that time largely of slave merchants or local businessmen who catered to them—and the commander of the army, as well as with the bishop and the chief justice of the colony. Below the governor military commanders administered *presidios* or captaincies virtually arbitrarily. Each *presidio* was divided into chiefdoms controlled by headmen from the traditional leadership clans of each locality. Officials were unsalaried, so corruption was rampant. The principle of governance was to extract as much tribute—in metals, ivory, cloth, but principally in the form of slaves—as possible.

Slaves were garnered in several ways. Chiefs impressed local criminals and debtors to make up their tribute quotas (or sometimes, simply secretly sold such prisoners directly to the slave traders). The human tribute was then turned over to the *presidio* commanders who, after selling some for their personal profit, handed the rest over to the governor who sold them to the traders in return for money and supplies to pay the expenses of governing the colony. Many government and military officials as well as civilians were also privately involved in the trade. They organized and financed expeditions into the interior to buy or capture slaves whom they resold to the coastal traders. But most important of all, wars produced the greatest number of slaves. Rebellions (which were frequent) or invasions, or offensive attacks on neighboring areas resulted in captives. They became the property of their captors, who immediately sold them to the slave dealers. Wars thus became a commercial policy. Indeed the whole Angola colony was so consumed with the slave trade that little or no effort was made to develop other resources, much less reform administration.

Portugal's determination to open the eastern Atlantic and the route to India thus resulted in two novel experiments in Euro-African relations. One died immediately and the other remained moribund for three hundred years, only to be rivived. The initially cooperative and mutually profitable cultural and economic intercourse between Portugal and Congo proved unique and shortlived, and was never revived there or elsewhere in Africa. Similarly, the Portuguese conquest and transformation of Angola into a colony governed casually and corruptly from the mother-country, though mmed not immediately imitated by other European powers, would become, in the latter nineteenth century, the accepted pattern of Europe's imperialistic ventures not only in Africa, but around the globe. The explanation of the demise of the one experiment and the long delay in the spread of the other lay in the growth of the international trade, development determined by events that were already taking place on the other side of the Atlantic.

CHAPTER FIVE

The Old Worlds
and the New

Portugal's successes in the Atlantic galvanized her neighbor and competitor, Spain—or more exactly Castile. Jealous and uneasy at seeing Portugal occupy one group of islands after another in her push down the African coast, Spain determined to have some of the new finds for herself. She set her sights on the Canaries, islands Portugal had claimed but not occupied, and wrested them from Portugal in 1475. She had made a beginning at catching up with Portugal, but had gained very little very late. Perhaps too late, for there were no more known islands left, only mariners' yarns about mysterious unexplored islands farther out in the ocean, such as Atlantis. But Spain was desperate and willing to try almost anything.

At that point Christopher Columbus entered the

scene. Columbus was, and remains, something of a man of mystery. Dynamic and persuasive in personality, he was secretive about his past and his plans. We do not even know for sure, for example, where he was born, much less precisely what he hoped or expected to find by sailing westward on the Atlantic. Most probably he was from Genoa and spent several of his younger years at sea, in the course of which he visited some of the ports that Portugal had opened in West Africa. He was not, however, a professional seaman, but a self-trained geographical theorist with considerable knowledge of navigation, though how and where he acquired his education and exactly what his theories were, no one knows. In any event, he developed plans for a voyage of discovery in the Atlantic and sought royal support for his venture from, in turn, the rulers of Portugal, France, and England. Each of the monarchs, after considering the plan, decided against it—not because it seemed too fantastic, but because they viewed it as an unsound investment. Portugal was already deeply and expensively involved in exploration of African waters through which she expected to find a route to India; England was just recovering from the War of the Roses; and France had her sights set on conquering Italy. So Columbus tried Spain.

Spain was interested, but her attention was largely taken up with completing the conquest of Granada, the last remaining Moslem stronghold on the peninsula. When that was finally accomplished, Ferdinand and Isabella agreed, after almost seven years' delay, to sponsor Columbus's voyage. Isabella named him Admiral of the Ocean Sea, agreed to all his demands for rewards for what he might find, and had three vessels outfitted for him. He set sail in August of 1492, stopped briefly at the Canaries for repairs, and proceeded across the Atlantic. After thirty-three days of sailing, marked by grumbling among his crew but nothing approaching mutiny, Columbus sighted land—the island of San Salvador—where he landed and officially claimed the area for Spain. Then he sailed along the coasts of Cuba and Haiti, where he bartered for some gold trinkets and took a few native hostages. Hardly had he put to sea again when a treacherous current wrecked his flagship and he was forced to set sail for home.

Once back in Spain he announced that he had found islands lying off the coasts of Japan and China and displayed his gold trinkets and his strange-looking hostages as proof. The Spanish sovereigns were convinced, but disappointed that he had found no real treasure. They immediately outfitted another expedition, this time seventeen vessels, and ordered him to return and find the mainland of China with all its riches. This second voyage of 1493-96 established a colony at Santo Domingo, discovered a few more of the West Indian Islands, but revealed no gold-laden shores of China. Columbus eventually undertook a third voyage in 1498 and in 1502 a fourth, both unsuccessful, at least from his point of view. In 1506 the Admiral of the Ocean Sea died still convinced that he had found Asia.

When Portugal learned of Columbus's initial discoveries of hitherto unknown islands, she immediately announced claim to them on the grounds that they were part of the Azores group which she already owned. Spain objected and appealed to Rome. Pope Alexander VI, a Spaniard, gave ready support with three bulls confirming to Spain all lands found west of the Azores and the Cape Verde Islands. Portugal was angry, but not willing to fight for what might well turn out to be only a few islands inhabited by savages. Then the pope added a fourth bull awarding Spain title to all new lands found anywhere, including India. At the mention of India, Portugal was outraged and alarmed. She hinted at the possibility of war and at the same time craftily approached Spain for a negotiated settlement, suggesting that a line of demarcation between Spanish and Portuguese spheres of influence be drawn 370 leagues west of the Azores and Cape Verde Islands. Anxious to avoid open conflict and convinced that she held the keys to the orient via the western Atlantic, Spain quickly agreed, and the Treaty of Tordesillas was signed in 1494. Portugal too was delighted because she now had clear title to the eastern Atlantic, including not only to the prized route to India that she was developing, but all of Africa, most of the south Atlantic, and, as it would develop, a goodly portion of South America. Both parties to the treaty got (and gave away) far more than they knew.

A New World

Within a few years Spaniards west of the line of demarcation and Portuguese in Brazil discovered, beyond the islands that Columbus had found, a mainland that constituted a New World. The New World was vast beyond comprehension and inhospitable at every turn. Stretching very nearly from pole to pole, it covered over 13,000,000 square miles of land area, close to a third again as large as Europe and Africa combined. Different in so many ways from Europe, the parts of it the Spanish and Portuguese first encountered more closely resembled Africa. Not only was Latin America shaped much like Africa, the major land mass of each assuming the form of a triangle with the apex pointing towards the South Pole, but both continents were characterized by pronounced differences in elevation from one region to another, a climate and landscape ranging from humid rain forest to desert, and numerous but largely unnavigable rivers.

Almost the entirety of the Americas lying between the Tropics of Cancer and Capricorn had a winterless tropical climate with little or no seasonal variation. The natural vegetation was a thick and tangled growth of broad-leaved evergreen forest that allowed little light to reach the ground. On both sides of the tropics were savanna areas, supporting deciduous forest and grassland. Interrupting the tropical climates were highlands in Middle and South America that furnished relief from the oppressive heat and humidity of the tropical lowlands. On the cool plateaus the aboriginal peoples developed their more advanced cultures, and here the European invaders, in time, settled. To the north and west lay steppe and dessert regions characterized by extensive alluvial fills, frequent exposure of bedrock, and scant vegetation. Latin America's rivers were scarcely more inviting. Those of Mexico and Central America were swift flood streams and the ones on the west coast of South America equally unadaptable to human use or benefit. Though some of the greatest rivers of the world flow into the Atlantic and the Caribbean, including the Magdalena-Cauca system, the Orinoco, the Parana-Paraguay system and the fabulous Amazon, they too have only limited use. Flooding, silted channels, and limited access keep any of the great river systems from serving the continent as the Mississippi, the Missouri, the Ohio and the St. Lawrence do North America.

New Peoples

The new-found world was peopled by an array of "indians" far more startling to the Europeans than black Africans had ever been. Europeans, after all, had for centuries heard tales about the "Ethiopians," artists had frequently portrayed them, and by the time of the discoveries quite a few Europeans had even caught a glimpse of a black or two, usually in the entourage of some great nobleman from Spain, Portugal or Italy. But for the sight of Indians, Europe was not prepared.

Though a few Indian populations, such as the Aztecs and Incas, lived in population centers and had highly developed agriculture, most were still in the gathering and hunting stage of cultural development and had nothing like cities. Most were still in the stone age, and none knew the use of iron. They had neither currency nor writing. Their trade was largely local, and true commerce was non-existent. Concepts of law, private property, and profit, in the Eurpean sense, did not exist. And slavery was so rare as to be incidental. Moreover, the sheer weight of numbers must have impressed the Europeans tremendously. Suddenly they had discovered millions of people whose presence in the world they had never suspected, though the early discoverers and explorers, of course, did not come into contact with all of them for several generations.

Spanish and Portuguese explorers and settlers found among the Latin American Indians a bewildering variety of cultural levels as diverse as the landscape itself. On the tropical islands and coastal lowlands of the Caribbean and in the Amazon Valley, Indian populations were small, settlements generally not permanent, and life uncertain. There the inhabitants lived by gathering in the forests, trapping the sparse jungle game, fishing, and occasional inferior slash-and-burn agriculture. In addition to these primitive peoples—particularly in the hills of the larger islands and in the varied environment of the uplands of Central America, the northern Andes, and what is modern Venezuela—there were somewhat more organized communities of Indians who maintained small farm villages. On the central plateau of Mexico and in the Central Andes of modern Peru, in contrast, there had developed large dense populations, tightly organized into large political communities and cities that supported themselves by intensive irrigation farming and a highly developed technology. On the geographic extremes of the continents—in the southern Andes, in northern Mexico, and on the North American plains, where desert and scrub steppes limited farming —only small scale pastoral villages occurred. In such areas the main part of the sparse population supported itself by hunting.

Even in the relatively advanced culture in Mexico and Peru, the population suffered from meat shortage, for prior to the introduction of European horses, cattle, sheep, pigs, burros and chickens, the Western

Hemisphere as a whole lacked wild species of animals suitable for domestication. A few wild birds and animals were sometimes kept as ornaments or pets, but only the llama, alpaca, dog, guinea pig, and certain types of ducks were genuinely domesticated, and they were always in too short supply to be used extensively for food. The populations lived for the most part on a vegetable diet.

Agricultural Attainments

There was no shortage of edible and useful plants, many of them rich enough in proteins to make up somewhat for the shortage of meat. Wild fruits and nuts were plentiful and the recurrent palm was especially valuable. From it the Indians took edible shoots as well as its fruits and, from the fermented pith, made wine. They also used palm wood for bows and what remained of the tree as a nest for the edible larvae or slugs that they used to help satisfy their meat-hunger. In addition they developed an impressive list of domesticated plants, among them maize, kidney beans, lima beans, various squashes, peppers, tomatoes, white potatoes, sweet potatoes, peanuts, manioc, and a large number of fruits and nuts such as pineapples, papaya, avocados, guavas and cashews. Besides food plants the Indians of the Americas grew special plants for medicinal or pleasure purposes: coca, the source of cocaine; mate, or ilex similar to marijuana; cinchona whence came quinine; tobacco; and barbasco, used for drugging fish in lakes and streams. They also grew gourds for containers, cotton for its fibers, cane for arrow shafts, rubber plants for the gum, and plants for dye stuffs.

In spite of such an impressive list of accomplishments, however, Indian agriculture by and large remained inferior to that of both Europe and West Africa. Indian agriculture as described was limited to a few areas of intensive bean and cereal cultivation, principally in Mexico and Peru. In those two places intensive cultivation and irrigation allowed a man to support a family for a year on a tiny plot not much larger than, say, a house and lot in a modern suburban development. Outside these two small spots on the hemisphere, however, subsistence remained uncertain.

Landholding practices among the Indians of Central and South America were equally primitive. The Indians of the Caribbean had no conception of land held privately. To them land existed only to provide the necessities of life—game, fruits and berries. It was never bought or sold or used for anything like commercial profit. In the high cultures of Mesoamerica, land tenure was carefully formulated and highly developed, but even here the land was never held individually. It was held by the village, the basic unit of settlement, and plots were assigned to each family. The family held the land as long as they worked it, but they could not sell or otherwise dispose of it. By the time of the Spanish conquest, Aztec landholding concepts had advanced somewhat, but not to anything like a private-property conception. Aztec nobles and priests were sometimes able to acquire large tracts of land for their own use, land that they worked with servile labor, not unlike Medieval serfs. But these landholdings were always legally the property of the village, not of the individuals. Such great holdings were relatively easily converted by the Spanish conquerors into private estates, or haciendas, thus establishing a landholding pattern that remained typical of Mexico's land tenure until the agrarian reform of the twentieth century.

But in the central Andes the situation was different. There arrangements did not lend themselves to direct incorporation into Spanish agrarian feudal estates. Though the Inca emperor held title to all lands, agriculture was basically socialistic. Some land was distributed in plots to families for cultivation according to their needs, while the rest was reserved for state or temple farms, from which the sick, crippled, widowed, aged and needy were provisioned. No one held private lands at all, and all work was performed in the collective interest of the entire community.

American Indian Society

Thus, in Indian societies no individual could amass productive capital, for it was all owned by the government or by the community, and no one could accumulate concentrated wealth, for there was no currency. Consequently, trade in the commercial sense hardly existed. There was little exchange of goods between close neighbors and even less between widely separated communities. Local barter consisted merely of exchange of family surplus and never developed into a mechanism for the distribution of specialized products in a true market economy. What little long-distance trade existed—and it was limited to the high culture of Mexico and to an even lesser extent Peru, for the undeveloped tropical economies were in no position to share in it—involved only salt and a few luxury items such as fine cloth, obsidian for tools, cacao, gold, feathers, animal skins, and precious stones valued as decorative materials. Jade was a particularly prized item to Middle American Indians, and some authorities have speculated on the existence of a sort of jade route running from the Gulf Coast through the southern escarpment to the central plateau of Mexico. But such a route in no way paralleled the Amber route across Medieval Europe or the trans-Saharan trade routes to Black Africa, for the American Indians never developed anything approaching a commercial economy.

Law in Indian cultures also remained largely undeveloped. Even in Aztec society it was more a matter of custom and accepted standards of behavior than formal codes. Restitution for the injured party was the chief basis for dealing with anti-social behavior. Fines and enslavement were not uncommon, particularly for theft and kidnapping. Individuals who committed crimes against the state—*i.e.*, by acts such as treason, robbery of grain supplies, adultery, incest, sodomy, assault or murder— endangered the well-being of the whole community and were judged by a council of each clan group and given punishments ranging from beating to torture, exile and death. In the Inca empire judicial development was even more rudimentary, limited to crimes against the state, tax evasion, and misuse of land. There was virtually no commercial or market law. Crimes, including any number of failings from laziness to homicide, were regarded as disobedience to the emperor and treated accordingly. Imperial officials, or if the infractions were of religious taboos, priests—there was no special judiciary—conducted trials of accussed persons in public with witnesses and meted out punishments, usually physical. Slavery was not used as a punishment, nor were fines, because the lack of private property in the Andean empire precluded them as it did civil litigation and property law.

Indian Slavery

Among virtually all Indians, including both the more primitive tribes and the highly developed Aztecs and Incas, there were individuals who might loosely be described as slaves. That is to say, they were set apart from the rest of society in a kind of second-class status. They might be prisoners of war who were spared scarifice because they possessed needed skills, or they might be criminals or traitors reduced to slavery, or they might be persons sold into temporary slavery by their parents.

Still others might have sold themselves into limited servitude in payment of a debt. Some slaves worked for individuals and others for the state, particularly in mines. Slaves, except for war prisoners, were not particularly suppressed. Aztec slaves could have families, hold property, or even themselves have slaves. What they lost were their "civil rights." Slavery was even less evident in the socialized Inca empire, though there were groups there who were permanently bound to serve a master or the state. These were often specialists—administrators, engineers, architects, or sometimes bodyguards for important personages. These "yanaconas," as they were called, were drawn variously from war prisoners, commoners, the sons of other yanaconas, or even from the sons of nobles.

Generally the offspring of such slaves, if we can call them that, whether in Mexico or Peru or in the less developed areas, seem to have been born free. Thus no permanent slave class was bred. Moreover, slavery was often a temporary status, endured only until a debt was paid off or restitution for a crime made. And slaves were not generally chattel, subject to re-sale, though there is evidence that some of the more primitive tribes specialized in capturing slaves whom they in turn traded for needed goods. Often these were war captives who served as drudge workers or, if female—as was often the case, for males were frequently doomed to ceremonial slaughter—they served as concubines. In any event slavery never achieved anything like the institutionalized status it had in the Ancient and Medieval worlds or would shortly develop throughout the Americas.

Land Without Labor

From the beginning the major problem for Europeans in the New World was labor. The European powers could discover and conquer the Americas, but they did not have enough manpower to exploit their new found empire effectively. Any time land and labor are the basic elements in a system of production, as they were in the early modern centuries, laborers emigrate naturally only when attracted by a better labor market. Such was not so in the New World, for during the early colonial period capital was always in short supply there while land was cheap almost to the point of having no value. In such a situation, exploitation of the new areas could be effected only if a cheap, constant and adaptable labor supply could be found. Because the colonists themselves could not produce the needed labor, it fell to the governments of the European states to procure it, if they were to realize the potential of the New World. There were other problems of course: how to modify political, administrative, social, economic, even religious institutions to meet the new needs. But these were all largely problems of adjustment and in time would be solved. Adequate labor supply was another matter.

In solving the major problem, as in discovery, Columbus was a great innovator. Once he realized that the lands he had found were not supporting a fully developed economy, Columbus set about finding ways of making them profitable to the crown of Castile. He envisioned the island of Hispaniola as an agricultural paradise, and from the outset discouraged gold seekers. He proposed bringing over European immigrants and settling them on common farms, founding a minimum number of towns, and establishing a carefully controlled trade with Europe via the Castilian port of Cadiz. Columbus proposed to pay the costs of the initial investment by selling Indian slaves in Europe. What Columbus did not anticipate was the official policy of the Spanish crown regarding the Indians. The issue of the Indians was raised in Spain immediately after the discovery, and in a short time Spanish jurists had issued a series of cloudy rulings to the effect that the Indians were free, though unfit to govern themselves, and that if they rebelled against their Spanish governors, they might be enslaved as punishment. Separated by the breadth of the Atlantic from close official surveillance and operating under such vague guidelines, Spanish settlers proceeded in fact to enslave thousands of Indians. If any production were to be achieved, the Indians had to be used as forced labor, for the Europeans were too few in number to carry out the job.

A cloak of disguise was put on Indian slavery, at least for a time, by the establishment of the *encomienda*. Recognizing the quandary of its colonists, the crown ruled that Indians might be compelled to work in agriculture, in construction and in mines, but that they had to be paid and that they remained free men. That is, they could be forced to work but they could not be actually enslaved. The *encomienda* required Indian chiefs to supply quotas of laborers, groups of whom were turned over to the European settlers to manage. But the subtle distinction between slaves and forced labor did not hold up in practice. The Europeans, responsible in every way for the Indians in their care, made them into virtual slaves. Once established on the mainland of Mexico, Central and South America (where it was called the *mita*) the *encomienda* system became particularly important and abusive in the mining industry. There it resulted in almost permanent exile from their villages for the Indians involved because of longer distances to work sites. The system would linger on in many regions until well into the eighteenth century.

While more and more Indians were thus in practice being enslaved, pressure was building up, both in Spain and in parts of the New World, against the practice. Isolated protests had been raised against the enslavement of Indians from the beginning, and by the second quarter of the sixteenth century these voices became a chorus. Jurists, moralists, and churchmen—Barthelemeau de Las Casas most famous among them —were demanding that the practice stop. And more than one pope had pronounced against it. Though simple humanitarianism motivated some of the protesters, many argued that the Indian was uniquely pure and undefiled by the evils that the Christian traditions had so long fought against. The Indians, to these minds, represented the embodiment of many classical and Christian ideals that Renaissance humanists and theologians were recalling to Europe's attention. Indians were seen as simple, honest souls, untainted by vanity, avarice or ambition, worthy more of pity and protection than exploitation. Unlike the infidel Africans who had stubbornly resisted conversion for centuries—Negroes and Moors alike, for the two were associated in the European mind—New World Indians had never before had an opportunity to hear the word of God. The Indians came to be thought of as a special case; they, as innocents, should be exempted from the penalty of slavery that could justifiably be imposed on Old World Heathen.

But in the end it was probably practical factors rather than moral considerations that determined the outcome. Indians were not good slaves. Indian slavery was rarely enormously profitable, and in the Caribbean islands it proved a debacle. Demoralized by separation from their families and the disruption of their traditional communal village life, Indian slaves fell into despondency. There were many reports in the sixteenth century of systematic abortions by desperate mothers, infanticide, and mass suicide of slaves. Moreover, the Indians had no immunity to diseases that the Europeans brought, and millions died from smallpox, measles and typhus. Populations declined severly everywhere, and in some areas, particularly the lowlands of the mainland and the Caribbean islands, Indians disappeared completely.

More important, even the Indians who survived were, from the point of view of the Europeans, of limited use. Because of their lack of familiarity with extensive agriculture, iron, money, and conceptions as private property, production for profit and slavery itself, Indians as slaves were, practically speaking, useless. They were not only unwilling to help the Europeans, they were unable to do so, for a cultural gulf separated the two peoples that was practically unbridgeable. The Europeans, then, had to turn elsewhere to solve their labor problem.

The Solution

The answer lay in black Africa. Special skills possessed by black Africans were precisely what Europeans needed to develop the New World. In other words, nothing like the degree of cultural difference that made the Indians useless separated the Europeans from the Africans. Most blacks, at least in West Africa, lived in villages, towns or even cities, were accustomed to complex social, political and legal organizations and a commercial and money economy, had considerable expertise in handicrafts such as wood carving and metal working, and had developed a sophisticated system of agriculture and animal husbandry.

Black Africans had command of a number of agricultural skills that proved particularly useful in the New World. In addition to importing grain from Egypt via trans-Sahara routes, many African farmers grew a wide variety of crops including citrus fruits, yams, rice, peas, beans, squash, watermelons, cucumbers, cauliflower, okra, peanuts and pineapples. They also maintained groves of bananas, coconuts, cola nuts and palms. From the latter they made oil, wine, vinegar and a sort of flour that they used for bread. Within a few generations after the discovery of the New World, Africans were cultivating some of its primary crops too, particularly tobacco.

Agriculture in many areas of western Africa, whence would come most of the slaves for the New World, was considerably specialized, some farmers growing yams, others, beans, and still others maize or oil crops. Farmers also developed systems of crop rotation to preserve and replenish the fertility of their fields. Such an agricultural system permitted the production of substantial surplusses over and above the needs of subsistance of the population and the support of rulers, priests and bureaucrats. Such surplusses gave rise, in turn, to a class structure that marked every phase of African life. In agriculture the class structure took the form of cooperative labor, usually organized in village gangs, directed by responsible leaders; in other fields of production it took the form of craft guilds of ironmakers, weavers, woodcarvers, merchants, potters and basketmakers, usually organized on the basis of kinship groupings.

Black Africans had also developed a kind of specialization of labor that would prove a boon to Europeans in the New World. Men did the heavy work, clearing fields and planting the crops or groves. If fields had been in recent use, this was a relatively simple matter consisting of breaking ground with short-handled iron hoes; if the field had lain fallow, the grass that had grown up had first to be burned off. If new land was being brought under cultivation, the task was more difficult, for trees and scrub had to be removed, the grass burned off, and then the sod worked. Once the crops were in, women took care of the lighter work of caring for them during the growing season and gathering in the harvest. Women also usually took the goods to market, sold them, and kept the gains in the form of cowry shell currency for themselves, often becoming independently wealthy in the process. The improved economic status of such a group of sellers, in turn, brought about development of highly disciplined organizations to protect their interests in the marketing process, particularly price-fixing agencies.

Concepts of Property

In West African cultures, where acquisition and ownership of wealth had for centuries been avidly pursued, conceptions of property were highly developed, again a factor that made the African far more useful to the European in America than the Indian could ever be. In theory everything in a kingdom belonged to the ruler, but in practice property was owned by family groups and individuals. No king ever tried to enforce his theoretical title to everything, though he might, and usually did, have vast holdings, particularly in slaves, as an individual. Each family group, the royal family included, also held certain property, such as palm groves and limited ancestral lands. But by far the largest portion of all land, wealth and slaves was in the hands of individuals almost as private property. Such property was sometime inherited, sometimes got by individual economic initiative, for the acquisitive urge was strong. Actual and token payments made when property changed hands indicated both the importance attached to the right of private property as well as liquid wealth in cowry-shell currency. In Dahomey, for example, when a new king was enthroned he made a token payment of a few cowry shells to individuals in return for assuming theoretical title to all land in the kingdom, and the king also ceremonially made a token payment for the war captives of each of his soldiers. Similarly, when a subject died his heirs ceremonially purchased land for his burial by presenting to the king a piece of cloth.

Some forms of slavery had existed in the entire West African region long before Europeans set foot there in the latter fifteenth century, and later, at least in Dahomey, a kind of plantation system existed characterized by absentee ownership that, by demanding the maximum return from the land, gave rise to conditions not dissimilar to those which slaves encountered in the New World. Slaves in Dahomey were an important labor supply, and yearly slave wars were waged to capture replacements for those who had died or run away. Whether the Dahomenian system was the exception rather than the rule for western Africa cannot be said with certainty, for in other areas slaveholding seems to have been of the household variety. In almost all areas large numbers of slaves were the property of the kings, for kings ceremonially purchased all war prisoners, the chief source of slaves, from their individual captors. Kings used some slaves to work their plantations; others they sold to foreign slave merchants; still others they set aside for ritual sacrifice. Kings sometimes handed over extra slaves to important men of the kingdom to hold, but the slaves remained royal property and could not be disposed of without the king's permission. Other slaves purchased outside the kingdom by individuals became private property over which the individual owner had complete control.

Given the fact that black Africans were familiar with trade, money and cities, and had highly developed conceptions of private property, profit and law, as well as at least some familiarity with institutions of slavery itself, it is little wonder that they proved attractive and able, even if reluctant, partners in the exploitation of the New World.

Even before all the difficulties inherent in the use of Indian labor became apparent, Spain was using black workers in her new overseas possessions. Accustomed to black African labor in the homeland, the Spanish government naturally thought of applying it in the New World and began, immediately after Columbus's landfall, to encourage the sending of Negroes to America. Some of the first blacks in the New World appear to have been either indentured servants or perhaps free domestics taken by their individual masters, but in 1505 a shipment of seventeen Negro slaves was sent from Spain for work in the mines of Hispaniola, jobs for which Indians had proved particularly unsuited. Soon black slaves were being sent for various tasks to Puerto Rico, Jamaica, Cuba, and the mainland. Demand for black workers increased as it became clear that they were far more useful than Indians, and in 1510 the Spanish Treasury sent out a shipment of first 100 and then 200 Negro slaves to be sold upon arrival to colonists. The Negro had become an article of commerce and the slave trade had begun.

Slavery and International Rivalries

Spain's need for black slaves was quickly exploited by her European neighbors. Their scramble to take advantage of the opportunity to sell slaves led to intensive national rivalries that testified once again to the profound influence that the black African had on the course of western civilization.

The first nation to profit from Spain's needs was Portugal. In the early years the Negroes sent to the Spanish colonies had come from Spain itself, where as we have already seen, they had existed in considerable numbers even in the Middle Ages. With the greater demands created by the developing trade in human chattel for the New World colonies, however, Spain itself was no longer a sufficient source of supply. Spain, having no African colonies, had to turn to the Portuguese who virtually controlled the commerce along the entire black African coast. The Portuguese merchants in Africa thus soon developed a huge trade in slaves for Spain's colonies, and grew rich from it long before they began shipping blacks to Portugal's colonies in the New World.

The Spanish crown, recognizing that its need for slaves constituted an enormously rich market for suppliers, early established a controlled licensing system for the transport of slaves to her colonies. This monopoly on the slave trade, the famous *asiento*, she had to sell to foreign companies, for no Spanish merchants had sufficient capital to undertake it. Certain enterprising merchants and sea captains who did not share in the monopoly seized the opportunity, usually with the strong, if sometimes silent, support of their governments, to smuggle shipments of slaves to the labor-hungry Spanish colonies. The result was a flourishing illegal trade.

England was among the first nations to try for part of the Spanish market. A powerful group of English merchants operating through such famous sea-captains as John Hawkins began illegally supplying slaves, along with other goods, to the Spanish colonists. The trade was deemed so important that Hawkins put figures of Negroes on his coat of arms, a practice followed during the next two centuries by a number of other English and continental adventurers who won fortunes from the trade in human chattel, including even some German merchant princes. The activities of Hawkins and other Englishmen played a large part in bringing Spain and England into open and lasting hostility. Shortly, the English government challenged Spain's pretensions to exclusive rights in the New World by planting colonies of her own in North America.

The demonstrated inability of Spain and Portugal to gain effective control of the American market invited enterprising merchants from other nations to try their luck in the slave trade as well. The French made an early bid for a part in the New World trade by establishing a colony in Florida that was straightaway destroyed by the jealous Spaniards. Thereafter French trade with the Americas took the form of buccaneering and piracy until the seventeenth century when France established another, more successful, colony in the Caribbean and planted settlements in Canada. France's lack of early success in her American ventures was attributable in part to her reluctance to undertake an overseas dispute with Spain, with whom she was already doing battle at home, and in part to simple lack of a strong and purposeful government during those generations. The French had also developed an economic policy that viewed overseas expansion and involvements as not only unnecessary for France's prosperity, but potentially dangerous. Hence France, at least for the time being, only incidentally entered the picture.

The Dutch were the most effective challengers of the Iberian monopoly. They had long been the chief supplier of spices and Oriental luxury goods to northern Europe, buying from the Portuguese and reselling in the northern markets. They now moved to their commerical empire the all-important slave trade, first by developing the trade in a colony they had established in Brazil, and second by supplying the Spanish possessions with black laborers. In the late sixteenth and early seventeenth centuries they determined to establish other colonies of their own in the New World to supplement their European trade and to supply slaves from Africa for their American plantations. Beginning in 1623 they launched attacks on the Portuguese colonies in Brazil and in Angola in Africa. They achieved temporary success in both areas but were soon driven out by the determined Portuguese. The profits that the Dutch made during the interim period were more than swallowed up in the cost of the war with Portugal that resulted, and the Dutch were in the long run effectively cut out of the American trade. But for a quarter of a century or so strife between the Dutch and the Portuguese for shares in the slave trade dominated the European scene. Thus the presence of black Africans in the Americas had, almost from the outset, far-reaching repercussions in Europe.

Spain's successes in the New World led shortly to rivalry in colonizing efforts. The Portuguese followed hard upon the Spanish in establishing colonies in the New World. For the most part the Portuguese were not agriculturists, but had become commercialized as the trade from the East flooded into Lisbon. In Brazil, however, they had no choice but to turn to agriculture, for Brazil produced no commercial goods such as the spices and silks that Portugal was getting from her outposts around the Indian Ocean. Even so, Portugal's approach to exploitation of her huge new American possession remained fundamentally that of the merchant rather than the farmer. Their delight was not in rich soil and bringing it into production, but in maximizing profits by organizing the labor of others and selling its products.

Lasting settlement began in Brazil in 1532 with the colonization of Sao Vicente. Building on their earlier experience with producing with the aid of black slave labor, sugar and wine for export on the island of Sao Thome and Madeira, the Portuguese in Brazil launched into sugar production. Sugar-cane production in Brazil was the great hope of the Portuguese, particularly after their initial hopes of discovering rich mines and local spices faded. It was a cash crop, the demand for which seemed insatiable. Indeed the soil and climate of Brazil were ideally suited to sugar-cane culture and the industry spread rapidly. The Indians of Brazil proved, if anything, less adaptable to the white man's demands than had those in the Spanish colonies. The Negro, whose worth had already been proved both at home and in America, was again the obvious answer. The crown made large land grants for plantations, encouraged the recipients to grow cane, and added such incentives as monopolies on sugar mills and water wheels to drive them. The venture prospered and the number of plantations grew rapidly from some thirty in 1576 to 180 by 1625.

The first shipment of African slaves to Brazil was made in 1525, though some settlers had earlier brought a few Negroes with them. The trade developed slowly because most of the Portuguese colonists, poor by Spanish standards, could not yet afford such capital investments and continued raids in the interior for Indian slaves. But Negro slavery increased with the growing wealth of the sugar planters and suppression of Indian slavery in 1570 by crown order. Brazil soon outstripped the Atlantic islands as the great colony of settlement for the Portuguese.

The English In North America

When, in 1607, the English began planting colonies in America, they found themselves faced with the same kinds of problems that had plagued the earlier Spanish and Portuguese settlers: an unfamiliar and hostile environment, strange new diseases, and isolation from the Old World civilization of which they were a part. Though land was plentiful and cheap, and could be made to pay handsomely from cash crops for export, labor was a persistent problem. Even for landowners with considerable capital—and by no means all had much capital, for land was relatively easy to acquire without it—there were few workers to be hired. The few from the wage-earning classes who could afford to pay the cost of emigrating to America sought higher situations in life than the ones they left behind. Underpopulation remained for nearly three hundred years one of North America's pressing problems.

Like the earlier Spanish and Portuguese settlers on the Caribbean islands and in Central and South America, the English colonists cast an opportunistic eye at the Indians. But the North American settlers found Indian labor as difficult to deal with as their Iberian predecessors had. Indeed, more so. From the outset the English experience with Indians was different in significant particulars from that of the Spanish. To begin with, the English were not surprised to find Indians when they arrived; they had known of their existence for over a century before they established colonies in the New World. Before they planted their first colony, the English, perhaps building on Spanish and Portuguese experience, had already decided to Christianize the Indians and teach them the rudiments of European civilization—something that had taken the Spanish and Portuguese some time to decide after their initial encounter with America's native inhabitants. But the English were surprised to find the North American Indians different from the Central and South American Indians they had heard about from the Spanish and Portuguese. North American Indians were more primitive, hence in almost every way even less manageable and less adaptable—impossible, in any practical sense, to utilize.

For the Indian populations of northeastern North America, hunting fishing and gathering wild foods were still basic to life even at the time of the coming of the English, though the Indians had supplemented these life-sustaining activities with meager slash-and-burn agriculture, growing some corn, squash, beans and pumpkins. Some of the Indians, such as the Hurons, lived in more or less permanent villages and towns having as many as two hundred dwellings housing 4,000 to 6,000 people. Most, however, remained semi-nomadic, frequently moving their villages and towns in quest of game and fertile lands. Political organization was primitive.

The Indians of North America

North American Indians knew neither real trade nor real currency, nor did they understand the private ownership of land, an idea particularly precious to the English colonists. There was some exchange of rare or necessary items, but it was carried on by a sort of relay process rather than through any genuine trade network. Furs, tobacco, some copper—which they beat into shape cold, for they never developed a knowledge of smelting—hemp and salt found their way over long distances, but the exchange was always small-scale and without a profit motive. Wampum (sea shells cut, drilled and strung like beads) was a much valued commodity that served as both a ceremonial item and a kind of medium of exchange, but it never developed into a genuine currency as cowry shell did in Africa. Private ownership of land in the European sense, generally speaking, did not exist among North American Indians any more than it did among their brethren to the south. Land—hunting grounds, fishing sites, and trapping areas—was thought of as belonging to the group, though parcels of it might be fished or hunted exclusively by a single family or an individual at a time. Farmlands were almost always held and worked in common by tribal groups. Only personal items, including moveable houses, were thought of as owned by individuals or families.

Though the English settlers early enslaved some Indians, the practice proved generally unsatisfactory, and Indian slavery shortly became insignificant in North America. Not only were the primitive and no-madic North American Indians, who had no institutions of slavery of their own, even less useful as slaves than those of Central and South America, their political organization was, in some cases, so loose as to make them unmanageable as a group; others formed so tight a political organization (as was the case with the several Indian nations) as to make them dangerous antagonists. Thus while the Spanish had been able to assume control of the native populations relatively easily by absorbing the highly structured native political and legal systems into their colonial regime, the English found themselves more often than not dealing through diplomatic bribes or outright force of arms with a wide variety of hostile tribal groupings. It quickly became obvious that it was not only impractical but foolhardy to try to hold as slaves Indians whose brothers were lurking in the nearby wilds. Such concerns early prompted the colonists to begin sending Indian captives to the Spanish West Indies where they could be exchanged for Negroes, a much safer and, as it proved out, more dependable and useful, hence profitable, labor force.

Black Slaves for North America

Though the first shipment of Negroes to England's New World colonies landed in Virginia in 1619, it was not there but in the West Indies that the institution of black slavery first developed amongst English settlers. Within fifty years after the West Indies islands were first settled in the 1620's, burgeoning sugar plantations required the importation of thousands of Negroes in order to insure a steady supply of cheap, easy to maintain and replace labor. By 1660, for example, Negroes outnumbered whites in Barbados. The conception and the institution of slavery developed rapidly in the islands with little trace of hesitation or misgivings, a result perhaps of the proximity to the Spanish and Portuguese colonies with their already long established black slavery systems. By the 1630's legal authorities had ruled that Negro and Indian workers brought into the islands should serve for life, while European workers might be freed once they had worked off their indebtedness. The idea of holding Negroes for life most likely was gleaned from the Spanish and Portuguese neighbors, for it was certainly a long time coming to the other English on mainland North America.

Though there was a trickle of blacks into the English colonies on the mainland after 1619, the conception of holding them as permanent slaves was slow to develop. Historians have not been able to reconstruct very precisely the early steps leading to acceptance of the idea of slavery because of the scarcity of records, but central to the problem was the fact that English settlers, unlike their Spanish and Portuguese counterparts, inherited little of a traditon of slavery from their motherland. Certainly the English had a word "slave" in their language and they associated a group of ideas with the word. But, rather like the twentieth-century man who still has the word in his vocabulary but no slaves around, the sixteenth-century Englishmen's ideas of slavery were somewhat vague. To them slavery was inseparable from evil, having originated in God's punishment of the sons of Ham for prurient disobedience. Hence a slave was a lesser order of human, one to be treated as a beast or, to put it another way, as the simple-minded and the insane were treated, as objects of scorn and ridicule. Slaves were also generally thought of as captives; slavery was the lot of the loser in a contest of power. And they were usually assumed to be infidels or heathens. This cluster of ideas constituting the English conception of slavery was to have, as we shall see, a considerable bearing on the development of slavery in North America.

Though sixteenth-century Englishmen had notions about "slavery," they had no slaves. Medieval England had serfs, of course, but by the sixteenth century they had been freed there as they had in most of the rest of Europe. In the isolated cases, always in remote and backward areas, where a few people were still somehow bound to the soil on which they lived or remained in the service of the master whom they served, their status was more a legal technicality than a condition of life. And such cases were regarded by contemporaries as oddities, anachronistic vestiges of a long-dead feudal regime. By the sixteenth century personal freedom was thought of as the normal status of all Englishmen.

Nevertheless, the late Medieval crisis in the fourteenth and fifteenth centuries had fostered the development of conceptions of compulsory labor and indentured servitude, both of which had profound effects in the North American colonies. The peasants' and workers' revolts that convulsed England and the rest of Europe in the fourteenth century as a result of ecological crisis, economic exhaustion, political bankruptcy and epidemics of plague, were crushed by the authorities, and the lower classes were subjected to rigorous labor laws. Vagrancy and idleness were mercilessly punished with whippings, brandings and various forms of forced labor that included a kind of temporary enslavement. But such solutions did not sit well with Englishmen, and problems of regulating labor continued to be debated in English courts and parliaments throughout the sixteenth century.

The Rise of Indentured Servants

By around 1600 the jurists and lawmakers had agreed upon the legal framework for a labor system that permitted compulsion but did not allow the total loss of freedom, conceptions out of which New World slavery would soon develop. Individuals might enter into contractual arrangements whereby they obligated themselves and their labor to a "master" for a fixed period of time. Many such arrangements were in the nature of apprenticeships under which a young man was fed, housed, and trained in a particular skill by a master craftsman, say, a carpenter, a barber or a silversmith, in exchange for serving as an unpaid helper for a period of a few years. Another arrangement, usually involving less lighly skilled labor and less technical training, was indenture. An individual might negotiate a contract obligating him to work, in whatever capacity, say a household servant or farm hand, or if he had the training, as a mason or even bookkeeper or children's tutor, for a "master" for a stated length of time. The "master" compensated his indentured servant at the outset by paying off his debts, bailing him out of jail, or furnishing him transportation to the New World.

Indentured servitude proved particularly adaptable to needs in America. Large numbers of settlers came to the colonies as indentured servants bound by contract to serve a master for a number of years as repayment for their passage across the Atlantic. An indenture contract could be sold or traded by the master, thereby transferring the labor obligation and, in the process, the person of the indentured servant to another master. The contracts were recognized in law and the servants protected from abuse at the hands of masters and unreasonably long terms of servitude. They were required to obey their masters in all things and perform assigned work. Masters were required to feed and clothe their servants and, in most cases, provide "freedom dues"—some clothing, provisions, and perhaps a small cash sum—upon expiration of the contract. Such arrangements provided a good supply of relatively cheap, trained, controllable labor that went far towards turning the wilderness continent into a profit-producing region. But the weakness of the arrangement was that the labor was all short-term, and some of it of even shorter duration than expected, for indentured servants frequently ran away. Some took up lives of their own on the wilderness frontier; others, particularly if they were white, simply moved to a neighboring area and blended into the community; still others joined Indian tribes. What was needed was long-term labor that could be easily identified and controlled, and, in time, black slaves provided that.

The development of black slavery out of or alongside indentured servitude is extremely difficult, indeed almost impossible, to trace because the two were for a long time inextricably intertwined, probably indistinguishable even to contemporaries. The best places to examine the development of the conception of slavery are Virginia and Maryland, the tobacco-growing colonies, for slavery was never of more than negligible importance in New England and was transplanted as a full-grown institution to the Carolinas later and to Georgia still later.

The development of slavery in Virginia and Maryland can be broken for convenience into three rough periods. From the first introduction of blacks until about 1640 is a hazy period for which there is very little hard historical evidence upon which to base conclusions. We do not know, for example, how the first blacks to arrive in 1619 were viewed, how they were treated, how they were legally defined, or even what happened to them. We only know that a Dutch ship brought them in and "sold" them to the colonists. We are not even sure what "sold" meant in this case. Were they sold as indentured servants for a fixed term of servitude? Or were they sold as indentured servants for life? Or were they sold as "slaves" as the contemporary English colonists conceived that term? We simply do not know. The only thing we can say with some certainty about Negroes in the colonies during these first two decades or so is that Negroes were distinguished from non-Negroes. That is, records from the time show that blacks were set apart from whites by the word "Negro." Exactly what this distinction meant to the early seventeenth-century English colonist we cannot say. Given the current English conception of "slavery" and their knowledge of Portuguese and Spanish black African slavery and similar development in the English West Indies, the Negro's status was probably never the same as that of white servants. But we do not know for sure.

Development of Firm Attitudes to Slavery

A second stage in the development of black slavery in the English colonies began around 1640. Between that date and 1660 more and more of the attitudes of what would soon become the accepted notion of slavery began to appear. Some blacks were being required to serve lifetime indentures, though without very exact legal definition, and were being called, more or less casually "slaves." And, increasingly, perplexing cases came before the courts questioning the legal status of mulatto children born of a black "slave" mother and a white father. During the same period, however, other Negroes were serving normal, limited periods of servitude, and still others were free, owning property and even "slaves" of their own. In general, these decades saw increasingly the singling out of Negroes for special treatment and debasement. The English settlers fell into the habit of contrasting themselves with black Africans whom they regarded, generally, as heathens. Needless to say, the dark skins and markedly different physiognomy of the Africans served to accentuate the difference. It was also during this period that laws began to exclude Negroes from the right and obligation to bear arms. Moreover, distinction appeared between black and white female servants. While white female servants were usually employed in domestic service, Negro females were set to work in the fields, probably because their familiarity with such work in their African homelands well suited them to the tasks. And, at the same time, feeling began to rise against white Christian and black heathen sexual intercourse.

After around 1660 these tendencies toward lifetime servitude for blacks, social differentiation from the white community, and general debasement swiftly coalesced to form the institution of North American slavery as it would exist substantially unaltered until after the middle of the nineteenth century. As more Negroes were baptised, the old practice of thinking of them as a heathen group was gradually dropped. In Virginia, for example, a 1667 statute specifically outlawed baptising as grounds for a slave claiming his freedom. At the same time, the convenience of being able to distinguish them easily by their skin color grew in importance. It was extremely difficult to apprehend a runaway indentured servant if he were white, for he easily blended into some not far distant community. But blacks were easy to spot and track; hence they were easy to control as a group. By 1661 the Virginia Assembly recognized that some Negroes were legally bound to life servitude, and in 1664 a Maryland law specified that all bound blacks were to serve for life. The vexing question of the legal status of mulatto children born of a slave mother and a free father was settled by a Virginia statute in 1662 that declared that "all children born in this country shall be held bond or free only according to the condition of the mother." The same law doubled the fines on whites committing fornication with Negroes. During the following four decades a series of acts was passed concerning such matters as the capture and punishment of runaway slaves and white collaborators, the prosecution of slaves committing capital crimes, the inheritance of slaves as chattel legacy, and the freeing of slaves. Such laws gradually but surely deprived bound blacks of all their rights and began the process of restricting the right of the few remaining free Negroes. Thus by the end of the seventeenth century lawmakers in the tobacco-growing colonies had, following what their society had been practicing in a casual, quasi-legal way, formalized the institution of racial slavery in statute law. Shortly afterwards, in 1705, Virginia gathered together her various statutes touching upon slaves and made them into a kind of slave code paralleling those already in existence in Latin America and in other slave states in North America. So by the time the slave ships began spilling their black cargoes on the shores of North America with greater and greater frequency in the eighteenth century, the English colonists were ready and waiting to receive them.

Slavery in Latin and Anglo-America

For a number of years historians have debated the similarities and differences in slavery in the United States and in the Latin American countries as it developed by the eighteenth and nineteenth centuries. The first group of writers to undertake comparative studies of slavery began publishing the results of their work in the mid-1940's. They held that the law of slavery in Latin America and the attitudes of the dominant Roman Catholic Church were both significantly more practical and more respectful of individual slaves as persons. As a result, these writers believed, slaves in Latin America fared somewhat better than they did in English North America where slave codes were harsher and the protective Roman Church largely absent. More recently however, after reviewing the evidence and undertaking new investigations, other scholars have concluded that such was not the case. They maintain that Latin American slavery was no less harsh than that in North America, and was, indeed, for a long period of time, more de-humanizing, or, at least, more de-socializing.

On balance, the most recent research—though one should always keep in mind that new discoveries might change the picture in the future—indicate that law and the church did not protect Latin American slaves any more or afford them any better treatment than that received by their North American counterparts. In both Latin and Anglo-America slaves were legally defined simultaneously as human beings and pieces of property. Statutes spelled out the place of slaves in the legal system accorded them, as human beings, certain basic protections against mistreatment and unreasonable punishments, and made them responsible, as individuals, for crimes. Moreover, there seems to have been little difference, in practice, between enforcement of the laws in Latin and in Anglo-America. Some slave holders—usually those living in sparsely settled frontier areas—were beyond the reach of the law in both places, and in such isolated condition slaves were sometimes subjected to the most arbitrary and cruel treatment. But in most socialized areas, and particularly in cities, slaves found some, though minimal, comfort and protection in the law.

Neither in Latin nor in Anglo-America did the religious establishments manifest much interest in protecting the humanity of slaves. In fact, religion—both the Protestant and Catholic varieties—was used to support, not weaken, the institution of slavery. Missionary efforts among slaves in Anglo-America were relatively limited in the eighteenth century, and when conversions did occur, statutes, as we have already seen in the case of Virginia, early made clear that baptism was no bar to continued enslavement. A far larger proportion of slaves was baptised in Latin America, for the Roman Catholic Church had long supported active missionary work among the Negroes, but the newly inculcated virtues of humility along with the practice of Confession quickly came to serve as an antidote to insurrection and an opiate for the slave masses. And though churches in both Latin and Anglo-America recognized slave marriages when performed properly as valid, such marriages were in practice little respected by slave owners in either place. Slave families were frequently split up by the sale of husbands, wives or children.

Further Comparisons between North and South American Slavery

But to say that Latin American slavery was no less harsh than that in North America is not to say that there were no differences in the institution in the two areas. In addition to minor regional variations in slavery practices within each respective area—variations among, let us say, Cuba, Brazil, and Mexico on the one hand and among the several slave states of the southern United States on the other—there were a number of more or less important differences in the institution as it operated generally in Latin and in Anglo-America. Many of these differences stemmed from the differing demands made by the economies of the two areas.

In Anglo-America slaves were used almost exclusively in agriculture, and hardly at all in mining, industry and crafts, for there were usually enough white workers and craftsmen to fill these needs. Slaves were used mainly in the cultivation of tobacco and, later, cotton, and only to a lesser extent in other crops such as indigo, rice and sugar cane. Both principal crops, tobacco and cotton, require relatively light field labor—sowing, thinning, transplanting, ploughing, weeding, cropping or picking—and still lighter finishing labor—stringing, curing, packing, or picking (or after 1793, ginning). Much of the labor required by both crops could be as profitably, if not more profitably, done by women, and even children, as by men. So, from the beginning, Anglo-American slaveowners were anxious to procure female as well as male slaves. Early records show that they were willing to pay almost as much for females as for males. Having both male and female slaves, moreover, owners would reap the added benefit of natural progeny. This led to slave families, and in time it became both easy and wise to socialize the slaves, that is, to teach them the rudiments of white men's ways. And still more important in the long run, the profitability of owning slave families probably accounts in a large way for the failure of manumission, emancipation, and the right of a slave to purchase his own freedom to develop in the United States.

In Latin America the situation was quite different. There the demand was for slaves to work in sugar cane cultivation, cattle-ranching, mining, and to a considerable extent, crafts such as ironworking, for the Spanish and Portuguese colonies suffered a chronic shortage of skilled free labor. Females were unsuited for cutting cane, punching cattle, or working in gold and silver mines, much less blacksmithing. As a result, their importation was discouraged, and Latin American slavery remained, for a long time, largely an institution of males. Records show that one Cuban sugar plantation having, for example, 700 male slaves and no females. Latin American slave owners found it cheaper to buy slaves from Africa than to breed them. Similarly, they found it cheaper to work their males until they dropped, then purchase new ones rather than to maintain them in good health with decent housing and diet. Moreover, there was no reason to acculturate a gang of male slaves who were going to die off soon anyway only to be replaced by a new shipment equally short-lived. So slaves were often kept in isolation, frequently forced to wear iron or tin masks to keep them from eating or drinking, and generally abominably treated. Hence the fantastically high slave mortality in Latin America—including many suicides—and the almost total lack of socialization, as well as the frequent runaways and the violent slave insurrections in that area of the world.

Free Black Populations

Not all Negroes in either Latin or Anglo-America were slaves. Some were outside the slave institutions from the beginning, while others gained free status after serving as slaves. There were a few free Negroes in the United States throughout the colonial period, and the number gradually increased in the first half of the nineteenth century as some individual masters freed slaves, as more slaves purchased their own and other's freedom, and as more and more simply ran away. Even so, however, the number of free people of color was never large. By 1860, when their number reached its maximum, there were still almost six-teen times as many slaves as free Negroes in the southern United States. Moreover, the life of the free black was rarely easy in the United States, for his very status represented, in the slaveholders' eyes, a threat. Consequently, free Negroes were increasingly subjected to control by the white community. By the time the Civil War came, they were frequently proscribed from holding a long list of jobs, their legal status had deteriorated, their freedom of movement was severely limited, and in many areas they could not bear arms, assemble freely, or even visit their brethren who were still slaves. The free Negro in the United States was, in short, hardly free at all.

In contrast, some areas in Latin America such as Cuba and Brazil were noted for their large, productive, and more nearly genuinely free black populations. The size of the free black population in Cuba was accounted for largely by the fact that manumission, emancipation, and the right of purchasing one's freedom were accepted there as natural aspects of the institution of slavery. A slave might expect his freedom after a reasonable period in servitude or he might purchase his freedom at any time, even on an installment basis. From time to time, the government emancipated large numbers of slaves as a reward for military service in defense of the island. The free black Cuban community was extremely important in the economic and social life of the colony. They were active in every economic activity, from the most unskilled jobs to the most skilled professions. And they formed an accepted and functional segment of society, linking the free and the enslaved communities.

Similarly, the tendency of Brazilian masters to free sick and old slaves in order to relieve themselves of responsibility and financial loss led, in time, to the growth of a huge free Negro and mulatto population. At the same time, Brazil's continuing under-population left plenty of jobs —shopkeepers, craftsmen, peddlers, small farmers, semi-professional— that free blacks could profitably perform, jobs that were unsuited for slaves and unwanted by whites. As a result, the free black population soared. By the end of the eighteenth century there were almost a third as many free Negroes and mulattoes as slaves, and after the mid-nineteenth century free blacks and mulattoes outnumbered slaves two to one. It is not surprising, then, that free blacks not only prospered and developed a viable culture of their own but, as we shall see, in some cases were able to maintain substantial contacts, both during and after the epoch of slavery, with black Africa.

CHAPTER SIX

Reverberations and Repercussions

Reverberations and repercussions from the slave society of North and South America spread both across
the Atlantic and across the centuries. Not only did the
presence of millions of blacks determine, in large degree,
the economic, social and cultural patterns of New World
history, but it also mightily affected the development of
race relations in both Latin and Anglo-America in the
nineteenth and twentieth centuries. Moreover, the New
World slave economies had a profound effect on the
future course of African and European history.

Reverberations in Africa

The mounting demand for black slaves in the Americas
quickly affected Africa. The activities of slave traders on

the coasts of Africa set off a series of economic and political shocks
that spread steadily inland from the late fifteenth through the eighteenth century. Coastal states such as the kingdoms of Congo and
Ndongo to the south and the seaside principalities of the Gulf of
Guinea were, as we have seen, the first to feel the effects. A stage later
inland kingdoms such as Matamba and Kansaje in central Africa and
Dahomey and Ashanti in West Africa superseded the coastal states,
taking over the main part of the slave trade then—in some cases absorbing them as well. And finally, at the center of Africa, the great Lunda
kingdom in the eighteenth century surpassed them all in both the
volume and the geographical extent of its trade as well as in its political
power.

Kasanje, Matamba, and Lunda

Economic and political effects of the slave trade spread like ripples
from the coastal kingdoms of Congo and Ndongo into the interior of
central Africa. Impatient with the delays caused by the long drawn-out
conquest of Angola, and pressed with demands from Brazil for ever
more slaves, the Portuguese in the middle of the seventeenth century
established contacts inland, particularly with Kasanje and Matamba.
These two small states, situated on the eastern and south-eastern borders of Angola and safely out of reach of the Portuguese armies,
quickly developed into important middlemen in the trade. Such middlemen-states, acting as both barriers and links between the suppliers and
buyers of slaves, were a common development all over Africa. Only in
central Africa, however, were they so far from the coast; in West Africa,
where the Europeans maintained only tiny forts on the shores, the
middlemen-states grew up just behind these enclaves, quite close to the
coast. Matamba was raised to its position of prosperity and power by
Nzinga, who had been the ruling queen of Angola before the Portuguese
chased her out. With the aid of Jaga immigrants, whose leader she
married, Nzinga reorganized the kingdom and began supplying slaves to
her former enemies, the Portuguese. Similarly, Kasanje, founded by
immigrants from Lunda lands to the east, became a powerful commercial ally of the Portuguese, sending them more slaves than any other
single supplier.

The economic stimulus created by the opening of the Atlantic and
the consequent slave trade touched off state-building ventures still far-

ther inland. Near the center of the continent arose the Lunda kingdom. In indirect commercial contact with the Portuguese on the coast almost from the beginning, a succession of Lunda chiefs built, by the mid-seventeenth century, a huge and powerful Sudanic-type state and took the dynastic title Mwata Yamvos, the Viper Kings. These god-kings exercised control of their own immediate Lunda areas plus a large number of tributary states in what is now the southern Congo, eastern Angola, and northern Zambia. Throughout the seventeenth century the chief economic activity of the Mwata Yamvos was selling slaves, via Matamba and Kasanje, to the Portuguese. In the eighteenth century they diversified their commercial interests by opening trade with the English, French and Dutch by way of routes to the coast north of the mouth of the Congo, and at the same time began a lucrative ivory trade eastward with coastal principalities on the Indian Ocean. By the end of that century the Lunda kingdom dominated the commerce of central Africa.

Meanwhile the opening of Atlantic trade, especially in slaves, was having its effects in West Africa too. In important ways the European impact there, however, was different from what it was in central Africa. It did not lead to anything like the population decimation, the economic destruction, or the political annihilation that took place in Congo and Angola. The Portuguese presence in West Africa was generally slight, for local rulers guarded their sovereignty and independence tenaciously, some of them, like the kings of Benin, manifesting little interest even in the lucrative slave trade. When the increasing labor needs of the American colonies of England and France forced those nations into competition for slaves on Africa's west coast, however, things began to change. During the third quarter of the seventeenth century the French established themselves in the region of the Senegal river and the British on the Gold Coast; both events stepped up the pressure for slaves. If the small coastal kingdoms remained aloof or only partially involved, their inland neighbors seized the opportunity for themselves. As a result, there developed new states oriented to the Atlantic slave market. Of these new states, Dahomey and Ashanti were the most important.

The Kingdom of Dahomey

The most remarkable new state to appear in West Africa was the kingdom of Dahomey. It began to take shape in the middle of the seventeenth century around the town of Abomey which was about sixty miles inland and directly west of the Oyo kingdom. In 1620 the ruling prince of Abomey launched the first in a long series of attacks that he and his successors would make upon their neighbors. By the end of the century, Abomey dominated some forty other towns and villages and its princes had become kings.

The newly acquired legacy passed in 1708 to one of the most illustrious of the long line of kings, Agaja, who began to mold it into a nation. In preparation for further conquests, Agaja reorganized his existing army and established a military training program for new troops, including young boys who were carefully groomed to be soldiers. At the same time he organized an information-gathering and disseminating agency—a spy service—which supplied him with information on the military plans of his neighbors and foisted his official propaganda on his enemies as well as on his own subjects. His preparations complete, Agaja embarked upon expansion, attacking and subduing first the regions to the northwest. That area secured by 1724, he turned to the south, and by 1727 had conquered and annexed the weak and divided seaside principalities that were by this time nothing more than puppet-states of the European slave traders who were already entrenched on the coast. With the coastal area safely in hand, Dahomey was able to exploit the trade in slaves as never before, making it into its most lucrative enterprise for generations to come.

Agaja's successors in the eighteenth century continued his aggressive foreign policy, adding small territories to the domain on both its northern and southern frontiers. And in the nineteenth century, the Dahomey rulers succeeded in taking several provinces, along with their slave-trade contracts, away from the declining Oyo state, thus rounding out their kingdom which remained not only intact, but strong enough to stave off absorption by the European imperial powers until conquered by France in 1894. Though the most persistently powerful of the coastal kingdoms of West Africa, Dahomey was by no means the largest. At its fullest extent it was a long narrow state extending from the sea, where it was only thirty miles wide, inland a distance of about a hundred miles, at which point it was no more than fifty miles wide—in total area, considerably smaller than Switzerland.

Indeed, like Switzerland, Dahomey owed its longevity largely to a combination of military preparedness and national consciousness.

Building on the early military base laid by Agaja, its later monarchs made Dahomey into what one European observer called "a black Sparta." They maintained a large standing army—the best trained, best organized, and strongest on the west coast of Africa—into which they impressed not only all able-bodied men, but women as well. The king himself closely controlled all military appointments and made his army commanders ranking members of his official state council, thus insuring the armies' loyalty to the crown.

Dahomey alone among the West African states also pursued a policy of forced nationalization. That is to say, they sought to obliterate the local customs, laws and lineages of their subject peoples, and impose Dahomey traditions instead. Upon conquering a new area, the king of Dahomey immediately abolished its ruling dynasty—exiling or executing all members of the family—and appointing in their place his own governors who proceeded systematically to suppress local institutions, substituting centralized administration. The entire kingdom was arbitrarily divided into six new administrative provinces, their boundaries intentionally drawn so as to ignore older lines of community demarcations. Each province was controlled by a provincial chief who directed the activities of the regional governors and their subordinates, the local village chiefs. Moreover the king stationed a royal agent in each town to observe proceedings and make periodical reports directly to the capital, and maintained close communication with his local officials throughout the realm by means of a system of relay-runners. Even the composition of the king's state council (which aided him in administering this vast complex of sub-officials) reflected the policy of state integration. Besides the usual ministers for foreign affairs, war, finance, ritual, agriculture and so on, there was a special minister who had charge of controlling the activities of the Europeans on the coast to prevent their becoming a disruptive force in Dahomey as they had in other kingdoms and principalities. The general effect of the policy of Dahomenization, at whatever level it was applied, was to bind what otherwise would have been a loose heterogeneous group of various peoples and traditions into a solid homogeneous nation-state. This technique of nation-building, by refocusing the attention of all subjects from the local to the national level and specifically on their king, was strikingly similar to policies pursued by contemporaneous European monarchs such as Louis XIV of France and, somewhat later, Maria Theresa of Austria.

Subjects of the king of Dahomey, having no local royal dynasties to look to, were loyal first and last to him alone. In the minds of the people the king embodied the state in the fullest sense. His military political power enhanced—indeed, in a way, sanctified—by his divine attributes, he was an absolute monarch. All properties throughout the realm were held in his name, every judicial decision was subject to his review, all important rituals were performed by him or by his priests in his behalf. His word was law for all.

The kingship itself was protected from disputes and power struggles within the royal lineage by laws governing succession to the throne. Only princes born of royal wives during the reign of their father were eligible for the throne. This law automatically excluded the king's brothers and male cousins, usually his early sons who were born while he was still but a prince, and sometimes his posthumous sons, leaving, in most cases only a few candidates. Moreover, a ruling king had the right to nominate his own successor from among the eligible candidates. Thus, in practice, succession was generally smoothly accomplished.

With their far-reaching powers the kings of Dahomey commanded financial resources unmatched in West Africa. In addition to the traditional sources of revenue available to most monarchs of the area such as customs duties, imposts, tolls, fees—often paid at least partly in cowry shell currency—plus proceeds from royal estates, and the highly profitable slave trade, the kings of Dahomey enjoyed the benefits of a direct tax on each person in the kingdom, fixed according to the individual's rank, station, and wealth. The farmers of each village were also periodically assessed a tax on their produce and livestock—paid in kind—as were hunters, salt-makers, and the various craftsmen of the towns and cities. Supplied with such revenues, the kings of Dahomey were able to support and develop their central and provincial bureaucracies, enlarge and strengthen their armies, forcibly nationalize their subjects, and increase their personal autocratic powers sufficiently to hold out against pressures from European imperialists for generations.

The Kingdom of Ashanti

Akan peoples speaking the Twi language, who still make up nearly half the population of modern Ghana, were living around the confluence of the Pra and Ofin rivers, in the region west of the Dahomey kingdom, perhaps fifteen hundred years ago. Whence they came, no one knows, but they arrived there in a primitive stage and evolved their language, society and political institutions largely on their own, developing, by the fourteenth century, a number of small chieftaincies based on the gold and kola-nut trade that they and neighboring peoples conducted with the empires to the north. The early political communities were unstable and short-lived because of frequent regroupings and migrations. In the seventeenth century one group of the Akan, the Oyoko clan, settled a hundred miles or so from the coast and founded several principalities, of which five—Kumasi, Dwaben, Kokofu, Nsuta, and Bekwai—were the most important. From the beginning, these little states, ruled by kindred princes, cooperated closely with one another and eventually formed a union for defense against aggressive neighbors. In the union the king of Kumasi was recognized as the war leader of all the Oyoko peoples of the area. In the mid-seventeenth century, the king of Kumasi, Obiri Yeboa, began to convert the union of Oyoko principalities into a major kingdom by forcing several neighboring non-Oyoko peoples into submission and admitting them to the Oyoko clan, thus binding them into the Ashanti union.

The next king, Osei Tutu, who came to the throne in the 1670's, is remembered in the Ashanti's legend as their greatest ruler because he completed the conversion of the union into a state. Exaggerating the dangers of possible invasion from hostile neighbors, Osei Tutu convinced the rulers of the member states of the union that their only hope was to recognize him and his lineage as the permanent heads of the Ashanti people. This done, he assumed the title of Ashantihene—king of the Ashanti—and set about laying an ideological foundation for the perpetuation of the new state. The new king and his chief priest, Okomfo Anokye, effected a kind of instant nationalism by creating the legend of the Golden Stool. Each Akan chief traditionally had a stool upon which he sat when holding court—equivalent to the thrones of European monarchs. These stools were carefully guarded symbols of each tribe's solidarity and perpetuation. Osei Tutu one day simply produced such a stool—albeit an especially elaborate one decorated with gold—and had Anokye, the chief priest, proclaim that it had miraculously descended from the sky and was henceforth to be regarded as the royal stool of the new Ashanti kingdom. The people accepted the fable and the Golden Stool came to be venerated, as it still is today, as embodying the spirit and unity of the Ashanti nation.

Osei Tutu also created for the new kingdom a national festival which served as a further unifying device—the Yam Festival. Once a year, at harvest time, newly appointed officers of the crown and newly installed chiefs had to come to the capital at Kumasi to swear their allegiances to the king, thrash out disputes, and make plans for the new year. In the provinces the populace celebrated the festival with appropriate ritual cleansings, propitiation of ancestors, and homage to the Ashantihene.

The Ashanti kingdom, originating in a voluntary union, remained a kind of federal state in which the king's central government exercised only certain powers while the component chieftaincies—some of them kingdoms within themselves—retained independent authority in other areas of administration. The Ashantihene alone could declare war, it was he who collected tribute from the sub-chiefs and kings in times of danger, his courts were recognized as supreme, and he was the head of the nation. The national army that he controlled was divided into four parts (the van, the rear, the right and the left) with each member state assigned a place in one of the wings and with each wing under the command of the chief or king of one of the states. Assisted by his "Queen Mother" or "Sister Queen," a common feature of West African divine monarchy very similar to that of ancient Egypt, he exercised his prerogatives through a large bureaucracy charged with conducting his government according to the specific, and widely differing, relationships he maintained with each of the local chiefs and kings. The Ashantihene surrounded himself with an elaborate court that included, in addition to his administrative officials, special persons who spoke for the king to the people, royal stool carriers, musicians, umbrella and fan carriers, bath attendants, caretakers of the royal-ancestor tombs, religious functionaries, royal cooks and table waiters, shield bearers and executioners. Chiefs or kings of the component states of the kingdom maintained their own royal courts—miniature replicas of that of the Ashantihene—and their own armies. They were also the religious heads of their communities, had their own administrative hierarchies and court systems, and held responsibility, through their lineage, for the general well-being of their own people.

In the course of the eighteenth century, the Ashanti kingdom undertook a series of wars of expansion with the aim of economic aggrandizement. Conquests to the north, in addition to bringing into the Ashanti state great numbers of Moslem Negroes who not only went into government service but established Koranic schools in Kumasi and made many converts among the Oyoko, also gave the Ashanti complete control of the supply of slaves and gold that already flowed to the coastal markets. Their appetites whetted by the new riches of the coastal trade, they next turned to the independent principalities on the coast which had hitherto been reaping most of the profits of the slave trade with the Europeans. These small states, already weak and divided because of their separate affiliations with one or another of the European powers who were competing in the coastal trade, fell readily to the Ashanti armies, making the kingdom almost as large as modern Italy. The Ashanti kingdom, controlling now both the source of supply of slaves in the north and the coastal markets, was indisputably the richest and most powerful state on the African west coast.

The European Impact on Africa: An Estimate

The trade in ivory, gold and slaves that the European merchants had established on the coasts was a major factor accounting for the rapid growth of the kingdoms of Ashanti and Dahomey, but Europeans had no direct hand in their creation or in their political life. The role played by Europeans in West African affairs remained minimal throughout the slaving era. They held only a few coastal footholds in Africa in the form of forts—fortified slave "factories" or warehouses where the handful of resident European slave merchants kept their goods, both material and human. Fortifications were necessary only because of raids from other European competitors. Resident slavers had nothing to fear from local Africans, for the latter, acting as procurers of slaves from the interior, profited as much from the trade as did the Europeans. Europeans almost never captured slaves themselves; indeed it was rare for them to venture more than a few miles inland. Until the late nineteenth century Africa remained, for Europeans, the "dark continent."

But if Europe's political influence on Africa was not great, what of the economic and social impact of the slave trade itself? Even there the picture is blurred. Beyond enriching a few cooperative African kings and touching off a series of African state-building ventures, it is difficult to say with much certainty what other immediate effects the slave trade had. The introduction of new food crops from America, particularly manioc and maize, probably would have brought about substantial population growth had not exposure to diseases imported from Europe and the New World, such as smallpox and syphilis, ravaged the peoples of the continent. The trade also brought Africa the dubious benefits of European technology, for the traders flooded Africa with European- and American-manufactured goods—cloth, trinkets, tobacco, rum, knives and, most important, firearms. The cost, however, to Africans, was high. For the tradegoods they paid with the lives of some 10,000,000 of their countrymen whom they sold into slavery between the fifteenth and the nineteenth centuries. And who can say what the cost was in terms of destruction and death resulting from the panyar-ring expeditions themselves, not to mention the fear, anxiety and despondency that the new militarized slave-catching societies must have engendered in the populations.

Repercussions of New-World Developments in Europe

Nor is it much easier to estimate the impact of the opening of the Atlantic and the growth of a New World civilization on Europe than it was on Africa. One of the commonplaces of European history has always been that the great discoveries of the late fifteenth century and the consequent opening of the Ocean Sea revolutionized western civili-zation by re-focusing it. The Mediterranean, it is said, was reduced from a main highway of trade to a landlocked backwater and its adjacent lands withered to a declining level of prosperity, while Europe's Atlan-tic states—Spain, Portugal, France, England, and the Netherlands—grew to new wealth, prominence and power. Albeit in large measure true, the point must not be over emphasized. The change of focus required a very considerable amount of time to complete itself, and factors other than the opening of the Atlantic and the new colonial trade were simul-taneously working towards the expansion of western Europe and the decline of the Mediterranean lands.

As is almost always so in history, the inertia of continuity proved as strong, or stronger, than the force of change. Europe, as we have al-ready seen, recovered its equilibrium in the middle of the fifteenth century, after the traumas of the fourteenth, to launch what proved to be a remarkable series of undertakings. Government was enlarged and strengthened at all levels, particularly at the top; papal as well as aristo-cratic resistance began to be effectively overridden; and society re-

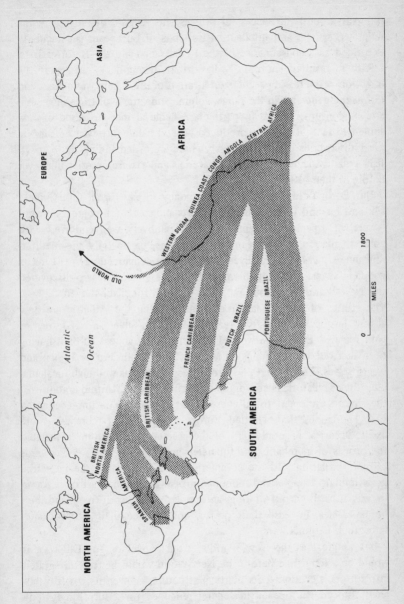

Where Slaves Came From and Their Proportional Numbers

grouped around the successful princes and kings. Not only were the religious, artistic and intellectual horizons of Europeans spectacularly expanded as a consequence of the Renaissance and the Reformations, but there resulted enormously important, if mundane, changes in the direction of increasing secular orientation of life. There was a great and far-reaching increase in the range, volume and variety of trade in general and of consumer goods in particular. Medieval men had used or consumed little that was not produced near at hand. But even before the great discoveries, Europeans everywhere were demanding more meat, fish, grain, wine, cloth, building materials and eastern luxuries than ever before in their history.

But Europe did not have enough money to pay for all this. Chinese silk and tea and Indian muslins, carpets and spices—all in great demand —were an especial problem. Although relatively well endowed with gold, thanks to her African trade, Europe, particularly the Mediterranean area, was short of silver. And the East demanded payment for its goods in silver. It was at this point that Cortez and Pizarro discovered the New World's fabulous mines, a windfall for silver-starved Europe. The stories of treasure-laden galleons plowing the Atlantic are now almost legend. Over 16,000 tons of American silver and 181 tons of gold reached Europe between 1500 and 1650, almost all of it having been dug out of the mines of Mexico, Brazil and Peru by Indian and Negro slaves. The impact on Europe's economy was well nigh incalculable. Indeed, historians still argue about the effects. Untold amounts of the silver were spent to purchase oriental goods on an unprecedented scale, purchases that whetted Europe's appetite for more and more exotic luxuries. A goodly part of the precious American metal inflated the profits of merchants and financiers and consequently went towards capital formation and the commercial and, eventually, the industrial growth that characterized modern Europe. And some part of it found its way into the hands of kings and princes who used it to expand their bureaucracies, increase their power, and finance their dynastic and, later, their national wars.

But as great as the New World's initial impact on the Old was, it would be a long time before the New World would be truly integrated into Europe's economy, its political structure, or even its thought patterns. Indeed, Europeans in general remained for a surprisingly long time relatively uninterested in the Americas. They seemed not to realize any of its potential or, for that matter, even the immediate importance of its silver exports. The latter is perhaps understandable in light of the fact that the study of economics was barely yet underway. But it is astonishing that Columbus and his achievement were all but eclipsed as Europeans continued to concentrate the attention, in rapt fascination, on Africa and Asia. In the century following the voyages of Columbus, the number of books published on the Turks and Asia far exceeded those on America. More astonishing still was the fact that Charles V, the man who personally profited most from the American treasure by using it to secure for himself titular possession of all of central and western Europe except England, France, Portugal and the Papal States, did not mention the New World in his memoirs.

Eventual Realization of the New World's Influence

Only around the middle of the seventeenth century was the Old World forced to come to terms with the New, to adjust its politics, its production, its trade patterns and its thinking to accommodate the Americas as a part of the emerging Atlantic community that would become, in the twentieth century, the focus of western civilization. The first step in this direction came with the breaking of the Iberian monopoly on the Americas in the course of the first half of the seventeenth century and the consequent effective establishment of overseas possessions by other European powers, principally the French, Dutch and English. This, in turn, opened up all kinds of opportunities to Europe's population. Men with enterprise, imagination and daring flocked to Europe's port cities to organize, as well as profit and learn from, colonial undertakings, while others braved the Ocean Sea in hopes of making their fortunes in the New World. In the process Europeans gained new knowledge of themselves and their own world as well as new confidence in their abilities to shape the destiny of the rest of the world.

The final step came with the increasing importation of colonial trade goods into the European market. Tobacco, sugar or molasses, fish, rice, indigo, furs, tropical cabinet woods, chocolate and coffee began early to enter Europe's markets from the New World, but remained small in quantity compared to goods of European or Asian origin. Towards the end of the seventeenth century, however, the demand for colonial goods in Europe began to increase, and by the middle of the eighteenth century such demands had reached a point sufficient to merit recognition of the colonial trade as a fundamental part of Europe's trade. The increased pressure on colonial production directly involved blacks, for, as we have seen, blacks not only provided the labor that actually produced a large part of New World commodities, but as slaves, they were themselves one of the commodities of the New World trade.

Effects of Abolition

In time, the influence of New World blacks was felt in other ways as well, most famously perhaps and most poignantly certainly in the movement to abolish the international slave trade. As sentiment for abolition began to mount, former slaves—both some who had gained their freedom legally as well as some who had won it by escape—proved themselves particularly effective spokesmen for the cause. Beginning in the latter part of the eighteenth century, ex-slaves went to Great Britain and the continent to present the case for their fellows still enslaved in America. In 1773 Phillis Wheatley, an ex-slave from Massachusetts who had established a reputation as a poet on both sides of the Atlantic, went to England where she was received in the highest literary, social and court circles. Following her example, gifted and less-gifted ex-slaves fled America to asylum in Europe in ever increasing numbers. Some ex-slaves came to Europe to lecture, some to write their memoirs, others simply to live. Sometimes their influence was great. In the 1780's Olaudah Equiano, for example, a former slave who had purchased his freedom in 1766, made a series of dramatic disclosures concerning the horrors of the slave trade before a parliamentary commission. Similarly the heroism of such black freedom fighters as Henri Christophe and Toussaint L'Ouverture in Haiti helped turn popular feelings against the slave institutions.

An interesting by-product of the abolition movements was the tiny enclave purchased on the Sierra Leone peninsula West Africa by a group of English philanthropists in 1788 as a refuge for freed slaves. By that time a great many escaped slaves, mostly from the West Indies and North America, were living in England, where slavery was already outlawed. Small numbers of ex-slaves had trickled into England over the decades, but it was the American Revolution that had flooded the country with blacks, for the British armies in North America had liberated them en masse and sent them back to England or to Nova Scotia.

In both places the ex-slaves were a problem. Though free, they could not easily find jobs or adjust to their new situations. Sierra Leone was purchased as a refuge for such ex-slaves and they were removed there. During the decades of the nineteenth century other former slaves, particularly those freed from slave ships captured on the high seas by British patrol boats, were added to the colony's population. As a result, Sierra Leone, ruled by England, became a melting-pot for ex-slaves, some having been born and bred in the New World, others having come, via brief periods of enslavement, from various parts of Africa.

Even with such efforts, however, abolition of the international slave trade was slow to come. The Latin American colonies opposed abolition because they needed the continuing labor supply; West African kingdoms opposed it because they had grown wealthy by selling their own and neighboring peoples into slavery; and various European or North American shippers opposed it because they were still finding the transport of slaves profitable. Great Britain took the lead in abolition, passing a series of laws against slave trade in her own port and possessions after 1806 and at the same time making it clear that she was determined to suppress the entire international trade. In the following decades she was able to negotiate over forty anti-slavery treaties with the West African kingdoms and various European powers. And eventually she was able, by using her huge navy as a kind of anti-slave patrol on the high seas, to pressure the Latin American area into agreeing to ban further imports.

Cutting the supply of African slaves had profound effects in Latin America. Despite the large numbers of slaves that continued to be smuggled into Latin America—as many as 30,000 a year in Brazil alone, for example—the general absence of female slaves and the high mortality rate of males meant that the institution could not be sustained at its former level. Mexico freed her slaves in 1829, Bolivia in 1831, and most of the other newly independent Latin American nations by 1855. The notable holdouts were Brazil and the Spanish colony of Cuba. In an attempt to provide the needed labor, owners there began to develop an internal slave trade, something that had never before existed on any considerable scale in Latin America. What few slave families existed were split up and their members sold off. But the needs could not be made up so quickly, and the whole institution went into serious decline around the mid-nineteenth century. Slavery became unprofitable and abolition followed. By 1886 slaves were free in Cuba, and finally by 1888 in Brazil.

Meanwhile, North America was also experiencing the effects of the ending of the international slave trade, but effects very different from those felt in Latin America. The United States government in 1808 outlawed the importation of slaves into the country. But by that time the trade had all but ceased because female slaves in Anglo-America had produced almost enough native-born offspring to meet the need for new slaves. Most authorities agree that after 1808 very few new slaves were smuggled into the country, probably not more than 1000 a year. In the course of the nineteenth century, states such as Virginia, Maryland and Kentucky, with surplus slave populations, became suppliers to the deep-south states that were still in need of increased numbers of slaves. This practice of breeding slaves for the internal market probably led to an even greater degree of dismemberment of slave families, as the offspring, and sometimes the fathers and mothers, were shipped south. Certainly it marked North American slavery as unique in the annals of history, for neither in the ancient or Medieval worlds nor in Latin America was slavery ever a self-perpetuating institution. Only in the United States was a slave population sustained primarily by its own progeny.

Native-born slaves, raised from birth to be a part of the system, were generally assimilated and retained little African identity. Their loyalties were divided between their own families and the families of the masters for whom they worked. Beyond their common degradation, they had little in the way of a common bond among themselves as slaves. Perhaps such dispersions, divided loyalties and socialization accounts for the relatively few slave revolts in the United States as compared to Latin America.

After Abolition: Africa As A Market Place

Even after the international trade in slaves finally came to an end, Europe and America did not lose interest in black Africa. If anything, their interest was intensified, though changed in its orientation. Africa remained a great marketplace for Europeans and Americans, but a different kind of market-place. Trade was still paramount, but its orientation as well as its commodities changed. Europe and America turned their attentions from Africa's coasts to her interior, and their efforts from buying to selling. Africa became, in the latter part of the nineteenth century, a marketplace, not for purchasing slaves, but for selling manufactured wares.

The second half of the nineteenth century witnessed not only the cessation of the slave trade and the demise of the slave economies in the Americas, but the concomitant rise of unprecedented industrial might in Europe and North America. New capital and new goods had to find new outlets, and Africa was a natural choice. Europeans and Americans were already familiar with her needs and tastes, they already had commercial and political contacts in her ports dating from slaving days, and they knew her weaknesses.

As late as the opening of the fourth quarter of the nineteenth century, more than ninety percent of Africa was still ruled by Africans, with European nations maintaining only a few small coastal enclaves. Twenty-five years later, however, all but a tiny fraction of the continent was claimed by European powers. The scramble for Africa was motivated largely by the opening of the interior of the continent to European industrial tradegoods, a feat made possible by revolutionary developments in transportation and communication—principally the steamship, the steam-driven riverboat, and the telegraph. Each European power with trade interests in Africa feared that its rivals would arrogate the trade of specific areas of Africa strictly to themselves by erecting high tariff barriers around their spheres of influence. Each power, therefore, felt compelled to grab as much territory as it could in order to insure itself that largest possible share of the rapidly developing commerce. Old notions of greatness and prestige associated with colonial empires and new passions of nationalistic rivalry also underlay the European powers' drive for African conquest. Moreover, late-nineteenth-century Eurpeans believed deeply in their obligations to "take up the white man's burden" of ending "heathen folly" throughout the world.

But it was not Europe alone that had an impact on Africa; the New World too made its mark. When the Dutch seized the Portuguese colony of Angola and made inroads in Brazil in the first half of the seventeenth century, it was Brazilian colonists and their Negro and mulatto supporters, with only minimal help from Portugal, who drove the invaders out of both Africa and South America. Brazil had saved the Portuguese empire from ruin, and thenceforth Angola was more dependent upon Brazil than upon Portugal. Indeed the entire west coast of Africa became subordinate to Brazilian interests, with even the military command of coastal fortresses in Africa subject to the Governor-General of Brazil.

Economic domination soon followed, and by the opening of the eighteenth century, Brazilian colonists had eliminated competition from the mother country and taken full control of the traffic in slaves as well as other products. Brazil continued to dominate the African, and even the Indian trade until the middle of the nineteenth century, exporting brandy, tobacco, flour, manioc and dried meat, and importing carpets, pepper, cotton, silk, damask, wax and slaves.

The trade led, in turn, to formalized relations with the African kingdoms, and between 1750 and 1811 several diplomatic delegations were sent by West African kings to Brazil. Dahomey alone sent at least four. The first of the ambassadors from black Africa to arrive in Brazil, said a contemporary account, was a "man of noble figures dressed in flowing robes and a velvet cape the color of mother-of-pearl and wore a plumed turban decorated with golden ornaments and precious stones." More surprising perhaps, was the fact that upper-caste Africans from the coastal kingdoms sometimes sent their children to Brazil to be educated—but, upon reflection, perhaps not so surprising after all, for this practice was roughly analogous to twentieth-century African republics' sending some of their youth for training to universities in the southern United States, something not unheard of today.

The Brazilian presence in Africa facilitated the transfer of many New World products, ideas and institutions across the Atlantic. In addition to manioc and maize, Africa learned the cultivation of tobacco, cashews, pineapples, potatoes, coconut palms, guavas, peanuts and new varieties of bananas. Other items that had originally been brought to the New World from Europe or Asia were re-exported to Africa, particularly rubber and horses. But the exchange was more than one of products—it involved the human level as well. Over the centuries, Brazilian colonial officials often went to posts in Africa and stayed there, as did many soldiers, civil servants, businessmen and political exiles But most significant of all, thousands of freed slaves returned to Africa to live. So many ex-slaves, great numbers of them having been born in Africa and brought to America in chains, returned to Africa that something approaching a pattern developed. This was happening regularly even during the era of slavery, as individual slaves purchased or were granted manumission, and it increased with general emancipation in 1888. Some went back simply to die in their homelands; others assumed roles of leadership in local African government, and not a few went into trade—including the slave trade itself. All of them carried with them what they had learned from their New World experience. As a result, even today, one can find in, say, Nigeria, such clear survivals of the colonial New World influence on Africa as colonial Brazilian architecture and ironwork, the celebration of New World religious holidays, and Brazilian proper names in great numbers.

But Brazil was not alone in treating with Africa above and beyond trading for slaves. Similar, if not so spectacular contacts were established between other New World nations and the kingdoms of Africa. The United States and Africa had, in a number of ways, a vital impact upon each other. Slave trade was certainly the major link between the United States and Africa before the Civil War, but even during that period there was considerable other commerce. From colonial days, when American ships sailed under the British flag, American traders were taking ivory, gold dust and dyewoods out of African ports. After independence, Americans extended their activities, for the French Revolution and Napoleonic wars had practically halted European shipping to Africa. In the second quarter of the nineteenth century, American merchants made great gains in western as well as in eastern Africa, where they came to dominate much of the commerce, exchanging cotton goods, gunpowder, hardware and other manufactured goods for ivory, hides and gum copal.

Out of the problems associated with the slave trade and slavery itself grew a remarkable American experiment in Africa, the founding of a refuge state for ex-slaves. This North American effort paralleled Brazil's activities in repatriating her ex-slaves to Benin and England's foundation of Sierra Leone. A large and influential segment of public opinion in the United States grew to favor the idea of repatriating both free Negroes and freed slaves to Africa. It included philanthropic-minded people, including some slaveowners who, though opposed to slavery, believed it would be even more inhuman to free their slaves in a society unprepared to receive them, as well as material-minded whites who viewed free Negroes as threats to their property, safety and prosperity.

In 1818 the American Colonization Society established a colony in western Africa and began organizing groups of returnees. The United States government lent unofficial help to the struggling colony, and Congress enacted a law providing that all slaves rescued by American naval vessels from illegal slave ships on the high seas be liberated at the colony. Soon as many as 4,500 ex-slaves a year were being landed. The colony existed for a number of years as a political anomaly, but in 1847, by arrangement with the Colonization Society, it declared itself independent and sovereign and took the name Liberia. Its captial was Monrovia, named for President Monroe of the United States. Great Britain, France and other European nations immediately extended formal recognition to the new state, and the United Sates followed suit in 1862, continuing its role as patron and protector of the new African nation it had fostered.

Missionaries and explorers from the United States also took a hand in Africa. The first American missionaries had gone to the American Colonization Society's colony of Liberia, and their efforts were soon followed by others who established missions at the mouth of the Gabon River. Still others set up stations in South Africa and, eventually, in the Congo. In addition, Africa attracted many adventurers and explorers. One of the earliest was Paul Belloni du Chaillu, a French-born naturalized United States citizen, who in the middle of the century explored vast areas of Central Africa. It was he who rediscovered gorillas and Pygmies, strange animals and humans that had been mentioned by ancient writers but subsequently regarded as fictitious by Europeans. The most famous African explorer of all was, of course, Henry Morton Stanley, also a naturalized American. In all Stanley led four important expeditions into the interior of Africa. His first and most famous exploit was his successful search of the wilderness, in 1871, for the lost missionary Dr. David Livingston. On a second mission, Stanley crossed the continent from east to west, explored the Congo, measured Lake Tanganyika and Lake Victoria, and discovered Lake Mweru, accomplishments that made him instantly world famous and established him as the greatest living authority on Africa. Stanley was then commissioned by King Leopold II of Belgium, who had formed the semi-private profit-making International Association for the Exploration and Civilization of Central Africa, to secure and open the Congo area for trade. Stanley's success in establishing trade stations and concluding treaties with Congo kings and chiefs led, in a few years, to recognition of the International Association as a sovereign power in the Congo. Shortly afterwards, events led to its conversion into the Congo Free State with King Leopold as its sovereign, an occassion that marked the beginning of European penetration and colonization of Africa.

Large scale direct and personal contact between Europeans and black Africans never existed in either Europe or in Africa. As dependent as Europe was on Africa over the centuries for gold supplies, no other African products assumed, before the advent of the slave trade, a major place in her economy. Moreover, very few black Africans visited Europe and even fewer resided there. Black Africa thus remained a vague and mysterious vision to Europeans, influencing the development of western civilization in Europe hardly at all in a direct way. Similarly, at no time before or after the slaving era were more than a few Europeans permanently settled in Africa south of the Sahara (except in South Africa). Characteristically, the contacts that developed between them and African populations were almost exclusively commercial and administrative, and were restricted to a handfull of individuals. Never were the populations of the two areas thrown into close contact. As significantly, therefore, as the economic and political life of one continent might have been affected by influences from the other—and unquestionably both areas were affected along these lines—in most other aspects the cultures of the two continents remained separate and distinct, influencing each other only incidentally. Certainly Africa profited from the advantages of European medicine, education, technology and perhaps religion, and Europe eventually became interested in certain aspects of African life—particularly art and music—but such exchanges did not bring the two peoples together. African culture remained African and European culture remained European.

Had early cooperation between Europeans and Africans continued, such as the short-lived early-sixteenth-century Portuguese experiment in Congo, the relationship of Europe and Africa might have been very different. But the development of the slave trade brought a quick end to such dreams and ultimately produced the opposite effect. Instead of mutual respect and cooperation, racism developed. Racism as we know it in the world today, while not owing its origins exclusively to New World slavery, nonetheless owes its essence to it. The growth of a huge black slave population in the New World and the accompanying slave trade represented the first instance in modern history of massive domination and subjugation of a different people. This was done, moreover, purely for the purpose of profit. Once domination and subjugation became tied up with the economic interests of Europeans, a conviction of superiority quickly developed. And once established, that conviction was easy to translate into a justification not only for slavery itself, but for later European imperialistic ventures in Africa and Asia. Black slavery must thus be accounted the most potent component of modern racism.

On the American side of the Atlantic, events took an important, if only slightly different turn. Great numbers of Europeans eventually settled there alongside the indigenous Indians in arrangements not unlike those that later prevailed in Africa. That is to say, the Europeans kept mostly to themselves, and the Indians, having proved useless to the Europeans as laborers, were left in virtual isolation. The developing New World culture of course had to adjust itself to such factors as environment, distances between settlements and between America and the European homeland, and the eventual mingling of various European national cultures in America. But the unique aspect of New World development sprang from the immediate presence of millions of black African slaves. Compared to the Indian, the Negro was, from the beginning, closely associated with the Europeans in the New World. Not only was his labor desperately needed, but his status as a slave required that he be kept close at hand. Consequently, he found himself contributing, as an effective partner, to the growth of the New World branch of western civilization. Dimly aware of each other since antiquity, Europeans and black Africans had, over the centuries, gradually come to know more and more of each other's continents and cultures. But it was only in the western hemisphere that they met in circumstances that necessitated their working and living together. And perhaps from that closeness, born out of four hundred years of reluctant partnership, future generations will be able to extract the necessary ingredients for a solution to what W. E. B. Du Bois, an American intellectual, himself a decendant of African slaves as well as Dutch, French, and Indian forebearers, saw, three-quarters of a century ago, as the central problem of the twentieth century: "the problem of the color-line."

Suggestions
For Further Reading

The subject of the present essay is not treated, as a whole, in any other single work. Certain aspects of the subject are covered or touched upon in some of the many general and specialized studies bearing on the histories of Europe, Africa and the New World colonies, but many aspects remain problematic, hardly, as yet, worked on at all. The following publications, most of them in English and many of them available in paperback edition, will serve to open the door and point the way for interested readers.

The Ancient Mediterranean

The basic work in English is the new edition of *The Cambridge Ancient History*, at present appearing gradually in individual fascicules many of which are pertinent to the subject under review. E. C. Semple, *The Geography of the Mediterranean Region; its Relation to Ancient History* (New York, 1931) is still the best thing of its kind and might be supplemented with J. M. Houston, *The Western Mediterranean World* (New York, 1967) and J. L. Myres, *Mediterranean Culture* (Cambridge, Eng., 1944) is an excellent short treatment, and Michael Grant, *The Ancient Mediterranean* (New York, 1969) is a book-length essay that gives considerable attention to agriculture, trade, and cultural transfers. H. d'Hérouville, *L'Economie Méditerranéenne* (Paris, 1958) is fundamental. Henry Hodges, *Technology in the Ancient World* (New York, 1970) is a good popular account. L. Casson, *The Ancient Mariners* (New York, 1959), W. Culican, *The First Merchant Venturers* (New York, 1966), Z. Herman, *Peoples, Seas and Ships* (New York, 1967), and W. S. Smith, *Interconnections in the Ancient Near-East* (New Haven, 1967) are all good, as are D. B. Harden, *The Phoenicians* (New York, 1962), M. Cary and B. H. Warmington, *The Ancient Explorers* (Baltimore, 1963), and the latter author's *Carthage* (Baltimore, 1964), the best thing in English on that subject. W. B. Emery, *Archaic Egypt* (Baltimore, 1961) is the best treatment of the origins of Egyptian kingship, and John A. Wilson, *The Culture of Ancient Egypt* (Chicago, 1956), originally entitled *The Burden of Egypt* (1951), is still useful though some sections, especially those on Akhenaten, are now out of date. Cyril Aldred, *The Egyptians* (New York, 1963) is a good general treatment based on archaeology. Henri Frankfort, *Kingship and the Gods, A Study of Ancient Near Eastern Religion as the Integration of Society and Nature* (Chicago, 1948) is perhaps the best treatment of the god-king conception.

On the early Greeks see R. Carpenter, *Discontinuity in Greek Civilization* (Cambridge, Eng., 1966) and for later activities A. G. Woodhead, *The Greeks in the West* (New York, 1962), J. Boardman, *The Greeks Overseas* (Baltimore, 1964), A. J. Graham, *Colony and Mother City in Ancient Greece* (New York, 1964), and M. I. Finley, *Ancient Sicily* (New York, 1968). M. I. Rostovtzeff, *The Social and Economic History of the Hellenistic World* (Oxford, 1953) is an old stand-by as is his *Social and Economic History of the Roman Empire* (Oxford, 1957). J. Rougé *Recherches sur l'Organisation du Commerce Maritime en Mediterranée sous l'Empire Romain* (Paris, 1967) is indispensable. Michael Grant's *World of Rome* (Cleveland, 1960) and his *Climax of*

Rome (Saskatoon, 1968) are sound general treatments and R. Remondon, *La Crise de l'Empire Romain de Marc-Aurèle a Anastase* (Paris, 1964) will prove useful. B. H. Warmington, *The North African Provinces, from Diocletian to the Vandal Conquest* (Cambridge, Eng., 1954) and Robert Eric Mortimer Wheeler, *Rome Beyond the Imperial Frontiers* (Harmondsworth, Middlesex, 1954) cover the question of early trans-Saharan trade relations.

The fundamental work on slavery is David Brion Davis, *The Problem of Slavery in Western Culture* (Ithaca, New York, 1966). It is excellent and indispensable but, because it is an essay covering the whole sweep of western history, it is sometimes difficult to use as a source for facts. Isaac Mendelsohn, *Slavery in the Ancient Near East* (New York, 1949) is a brief comparative study of slavery in Egypt, Assyria, Syria and Palestine, and the only thing available of that nature. Abd El-Mohsen Bakir, *Slavery in Pharaonic Egypt* (Paris, 1952) is based on a close reading of the sources with many exact citations but little synthesis. William L. Westermann, *The Slave Systems of Greek and Roman Antiquity* (Philadelphia, 1955) is perhaps the most complete treatment of the subject; it is filled with data, though some of its conclusions and especially its calculations of numbers of slaves have been challenged by later writers. It is actually a re-write of the article on slavery in the Pauly-Wissowa-Kroll, *Real-Encyclopadie der classischen Altertumswissenchaft*. M.I. Finley, ed., *Slavery in Classical Antiquity: Views and Controversies* (Cambridge, 1960) is a collection of published articles on Greek and Roman slavery but includes one essay on slavery in early Germany.

Frank M. Snowdon, *Blacks in Antiquity; Ethiopians in the Greco-Roman Experience* (Cambridge, Mass., 1970), a fascinating study of the subject that contains many photographs of blacks as depicted in classical art, is extremely useful though some of his conclusions are questionable.

Medieval Europe

An excellent introduction to the European setting is C.T. Smith, *An Historical Geography of Western Europe Before 1800* (New York, 1967). It treats prehistory as well as historical periods including such things as settlement patterns, peoples of Europe, agrarian structures, trade and towns, overseas expansion, and early industrialization. The classic treatment of prehistoric Europe is still V. Gordon Child, *The Dawn of European Civilization* (London, 1948) though some of its suppositions have been challenged by other authorities. See also his *Prehistory of European Society* (London, 1962) and *Prehistoric Migrations in Europe* (Oslo, 1950). Stuart Piggott's *Ancient Europe From the Beginnings of Agriculture to Classical Antiquity* (Chicago, 1965) is an excellent recent survey, up-to-date on all points, and has good photographs, line drawings and diagrams. Piggott also edited a popular work called *The Dawn of Civilization*, a survey of the earliest human cultures of the world that is interesting for convenient comparisons. See also J.G.D. Clark, *Prehistoric Europe, The Economic Basis* (London, 1952).

The basic work in English on the agricultural base of medieval economic life is the *Cambridge Economic History of Europe*, vol. I, *Agrarian Life of the Middle Ages*, eds., J.H. Clapham and E. Power (Cambridge, 1942). An authoritative survey of the subject that will prove both useful and challenging is B.H. Silcher van Bath, *The Agrarian History of Western Europe: A.D. 500-1850* (London, 1963). Marc Bloch's *French Rural History: An Essay on its Basic Characteristics* (London, 1966) and G. Duby's *L'Economie rurale et la Vie des campagnes dans l'Occident medieval*, 2 vols. (Paris, 1962) are both basic, and *The Agrarian History of England and Wales*, vol. IV (Cambridge, 1967) is excellent for the period 1500-1640. On the peopling of Europe see E. Salin, *La Civilisation Merovingienne*, 4 vols. (Paris, 1949), E. Levi-Provencal, *Mussulman Spain in the Tenth Century* (Paris, 1931), L. Mussett, *Les Peuples Scandinaves au moyen age* (Paris, 1951), E. Wiskemann, *Germany's Eastern Neighbors* (London, 1956), J.W. Thompson, *Feudal Germany* (Chicago, 1928), and J.C. Russell, *British Medieval Population* (Alburquerque, New Mexico, 1948).

On medieval trade and towns the fundamental English works are the *Cambridge Economic History of Europe*, vol. II, eds., M.M. Postan and E.E. Rice, *Trade and Industry in the Middle Ages* (Cambridge, 1952) and vol. III, eds., M.M. Postan, E.E. Rich, and E. Miller, *Economic Organization and Policies in the Middle Ages* (Cambridge, 1965). Both, however, should always be checked against the latest findings, for some sections are already out of date. See also R. Latouche, *The Birth of the Western Economy* (London, 1961). For treatment of specific aspects or regions see A.R. Lewis, *Naval Power and Trade in the Mediterranean*

500-1100 (Princeton, 1951), the same author's *The Northern Seas 300-1100* (Princeton, 1958), W. Heyd, *Histoire du Commerce du Levant* (Paris, 1911), G. Luzatto, *Economic History of Italy to the Beginning of the Sixteenth century* (London, 1961), and E. Chapin, *Les Villes de foires de Champagne* (Paris, 1935).

For the role of towns see F.L. Hiorns, *Town Building in History* (London, 1956); R.E. Dickinson, *The West European City* (London, 1951); E.A. Gutkind, *Urban Development in Central Europe*; vol. I of *International History of City Development* (London, 1964); G.L. Burk, *The Making of the Dutch Towns* (London, 1956); J.H. Mundy and P. Riesenberg, *The Medieval Town* (Princeton, 1958); and the older H. Pirenne, *Medieval Cities* (Princeton, 1949).

Ancient Africa

The best short guide in English to African geography, peoples and cultures is C.G. Seligman, *Races of Africa*, 3rd ed. (New York, 1957). On languages see Joseph H. Greenberg, *The Languages of Africa* (Bloomington, 1966) and the same author's "Historical Inferences from Linguistic Research in Sub Saharan Africa," in J. Butler, ed., *Boston University Papers in African History*, I (Boston, 1964). A convenient collection of articles and selections from longer works dealing not only with African languages but the problems of Bantu and Nilotic origins and migrations, the relationship of ancient Egypt to black Africa, the origins of African states and here continuing stateless societies as well as pre-colonial and slave trade is Robert O. Collins, ed., *Problems in African History* (Englewood Cliffs, 1968).

There are increasing numbers of one-volume general histories of Africa of which Roland A. Oliver and J.D. Fage, *A Short History of Africa*, 2nd ed. (Harmondsworth, Middlesex, 1966) and Robert W. July, *A History of the African People* (New York, 1970) are representative and reliable examples. Both contain useful bibliographies. For a beginner in the field the two small collections of talks broadcast by B.B.C. and edited by Roland Oliver as *The Dawn of African History* (London, 1961) and *The Middle Age of African History* (London, 1967) will prove fascinating. Between them C.B.M. McBurney, *The Stone Age of Northern Africa* (Harmondsworth, Middlesex, 1960); J. Desmond Clark, *The Prehistory of Southern Africa* (Harmondsworth,

Middlesex, 1959); the same author's *Prehistory of Africa* (London, 1970); and Oliver Davies, *West Africa before the Europeans: Archaeology and Prehistory* (London, 1967) cover the prehistory of the pertinent parts of Africa. For the origins of African agriculture and culture see Basil Davidson, *Old Africa Rediscovered* (London, 1959), a good short summary of Iron Age archaeology. The same author's *Lost Cities of Africa* (Boston, 1959) is a popular but usually reliable account of early Africa that might well be compared with V. Gordon Childe, *New Light on the Most Ancient East* (London, 1954) relative to the role of Egypt in black Africa. The best works on the upper reaches of the Nile are A.J. Arkell, *A History of the Sudan: From the Earliest Times to 1821*, 2nd ed., rev. (London, 1961) and Jean Doresse, *Au Pays de la Reine de Saba* (Paris, 1956). Consult J. Suret-Canale, *Afrique Noire, Occidentale et Centrale*, 2nd ed. (Paris, 1961) for arguments for independent African cultural origins. H.G.P. Murdoch, *Africa: Its Peoples and their Culture History* (New York, 1957) is provocative but should be used with care. J. Spencer Trimingham, *Islam in the Sudan* (London, 1949) and his *History of Islam in West Africa* (London, 1962) are excellent authoritative treatments of the subject, and C.P. Groves, *The Planting of Christianity in Africa*, vol. I (London, 1948) completes the story.

Probably the best introduction to the history of the western Sudan is E.W. Bovill's *The Golden Trade of the Moors* (London, 1958), which supersedes his earlier *Caravans of the Old Sahara*. Its main theme is trans-saharan gold trade between Europe, the Moors and black Africa, but in a total way it is a history of the region, and it is altogether a splendid book. M. Delafosse's three-volume *Haut-Senegal-Niger* (Paris, 1912) is the old encyclopaedic work on the area, but it should be complemented with modern studies such as J. Rouch, *Contribution a l'histoire des Songhay* (Dakar, 1953); Y.F.M.A. Urvoy, *Histoire de l'Empire du Bornu* (Paris, 1949); and J.F.A. Ajayi and I. Espie, eds., *A Thousand Years of West African History* (London, 1965). Works such as A. Adu Boahen, *Topics in West African History* (London, 1966) and J.C. DeGraft-Johnson, *African Glory; The Story of Vanished Negro Civilizations* (New York, 1954) are typical of the sort of popular and shrilly nationalistic history that is coming out of some quarters in Africa today. Even so, they are not without value, if used carefully.

Many of the accounts of Moslem travelers and historians, our primary source of information on the old empires of the Sudan, have been translated into European languages. H.A.R. Gibb, tr., *Ibn Battúta: Travels in Asia and Africa* (London, 1929) and al-Bakri, *Description de l'Affique Septentrionale* (Algiers, 1913) are but two examples. Convenient collections of short excerpts of travelers' accounts and inscriptions from the earliest times to the twentieth century are Roland and Caroline Oliver's *Africa in the Days of Exploration* (Englewood Cliffs, 1965) and Basil Davidson, *The African Past: Chronicles from Antiquity to Modern Times* (New York, 1964). On African art see Eliot Elisofon and William Fagg, *The Sculpture of Africa* (London, 1958) or Elsy Leuzinger, *Africa: The Art of the Negro Peoples* (London, 1960) for fine treatments and C. Kjersmeier, *Centres de Style de la Sculpture Negre Africaine*, 4 vols., (Paris, 1935-38) for fuller study.

Europe, Africa, and the Atlantic

A convenient text covering Europe's crisis and recovery is Wallace K. Ferguson, *Europe in Transition, 1300-1520* (Boston, 1962). The old standard in English is the *Cambridge Medieval History*, edited by C.W. Previté-Orton and Z.N. Brooke, *VIII: The Close of the Middle Ages* (Cambridge, England, 1936) which, though still quite valuable must, because of its age, be used with some care. Two volumes of the lighter American counterpart, the Langer series: Edward P. Cheyney's *The Dawn of a New Era, 1250-1453* (New York, 1936), somewhat old-fashioned especially in the sections devoted to the economy, but well written, and Myron P. Gilmore's selective work on *The World of Humanism, 1453-1517* (New York, 1952). The first two volumes of the *New Cambridge Modern History: The Renaissance 1493-1520*, edited by G.R. Potter (Cambridge, Eng., 1957) and *The Reformation, 1520-59*, edited by G.R. Elton (Cambridge, Eng., 1958) and volume IV of the *Cambridge Economic History of Europe: The Economy of Expanding Europe in the Sixteenth and Seventeenth Centuries*, edited by E.E. Rich and C.H. Wilson, (Cambridge, Eng., 1967) will prove basic. Jacques Heers, *L'Occident au XIVᵉ et XVᵉ siècles; Aspects économiques et sociaux* (Paris, 1963) is an excellent brief synthesis. The Cornell series furnishes useful brief essays on the period: Robert E.

Lerner, *The Age of Adversity; the Fourteenth Century* (Ithaca, 1968) and Jerah Johnson and William A. Percy, *The Age of Recovery: Europe in the Fifteenth Century* (Ithaca, 1970).

The troublesome problem of gold and silver supplies for Europe's economy is touched upon in various chapters of the volumes of the *Cambridge Economic History of Europe* already cited, while Europe's gold and silver exchange with Asia is treated by Andrew M. Watson, "Back to Gold—and Silver," *Economic History Review*, 2nd series, XX (April 1967), 1-34. And the gold trade with black Africa is admirably covered in Bovill's *Golden Trade of the Moors*, also already cited. L. de Mas-Latrie, ed., *Traités de Paix et de Commerce et Documents Divers Concernant les Relations des Chrétiens avec les Arabes de l'Afrique Septentrionale* (Paris, 1866; reprint New York, 1964) contains a long introduction outlining commercial contacts between Europe and North African states followed by a collection of letters and treaties pertaining to that commerce.

European contacts with black Africa are touched upon in some of the works just mentioned, but for travel accounts of Europeans who made visits to the interior of Africa see C.G.M.B. de La Ronciere, *La Découverte de l'Afrique au Moyen Âge, Cartographes et Explorateurs*, 3 vols. (Cairo, 1924-27) and A.P. Newton, *Travel and Travelers of the Middle Ages* (New York, 1950). Henri Baudet, *Paradise on Earth; Some Thoughts on European Images of Non-European Man*, tr. by Elizabeth Wentholt (New Haven, Conn., 1965) discusses the Medieval fascination with "Ethiopians," and the story of the black among the Magi has been traced by H. Kehrer, "Die drei Könige . . .," "Studien zur dautschen Kunstgeschichte, 53 (Strassburg, 1904). An interesting recent article that shatters the long-held view that there was in the Islamic world no prejudice against blacks is Bernard Lewis's "Race and Color in Islam," *Encounter*, XXXIV (August, 1970). The monumental and indispensable work on the institution of slavery in Medieval Europe is C. Verlinden, *L'Esclavage dans l'Europe Médiévale* (Burges, 1955). The author's pamphlet-size works *Précédents Mediévaux di la Cononie en Amérique* (Mexico City, 1954) is a remarkably good summary of European backgrounds for slavery as well as other colonial institutions. Spanish slavery around the time of the discovery is treated by Vincenta Cortés, *La Esclavitud en Valencia durante el reinado de los Reyes Cátolicos, 1479-1516* (Valencia, 1964) and Antonio Domínguez Ortiz, *La Esclavitud en Castilla Durante la edad moderna* (Madrid, 1952).

The best treatment of the discoveries and early colonial foundations is John H. Parry, *The Age of Reconnaissance* (Cleveland, 1963) which also discusses technical problems of seamanship, navigation, charts and maps. Boies Penrose, *Travel and Discovery in the Renaissance, 1420-1620* (Cambridge, Mass., 1955) contains accurate translations of accounts of early travelers to Africa. Charles E. Nowell, *The Great Discoveries and the First Colonial Empires* (Ithaca, 1954) is a brief but useful volume in the Cornell series. The effects of the coming of the Europeans to western Africa is outlined in John D. Fage, *An Introduction to the History of West Africa*, 3d ed. (Cambridge, Eng., 1962) which also has a good bibliography. John W. Blake, *Europeans in West Africa, 1450-1560* (London, 1942) and H.A. Wydham, *The Atlantic and Slavery* (London, 1935) are both very useful. R.E. Bradbury, *The Benin Kingdom and the Edo-Speaking Peoples of South-Western Nigeria* (London, 1957), S. Johnson, *The History of the Yorubas From the Earliest Times to the Beginning of the British Protectorate* (Lagos, 1921) and Robert S. Smith, *Kingdoms of the Yoruba* (London, 1969) are good introductions. The best brief account of Portuguese activities in Congo and Angola is James Duffy's *Portuguese Africa* (Cambridge, Mass., 1959), but for the African side of the story one has to go to A. Ihle, *Das alte Konigreich Kongo* (Leipzig, 1929) and J. Cuvelier and L. Jadin, *L'Ancien Congo D'Après les Archives Romaines, 1518-1640* (Brussels, 1954).

The Old Worlds and the New

Gordon Willey's *Prehistoric Settlement Patterns in the New World* (New York, 1956) is a scholarly treatment. *The Handbook of Middle American Indians*, edited by Robert Wauchope, 3 vols. (Austin, 1964-65) is the indispensable reference work on the subject. Robert C. West and John P. Augelli, *Middle America: Its Lands and Peoples* (Englewood Cliffs, 1966) and William T. Sanders and Barbara J. Price, *Mesoamerica; The Evolution of a Civilization* (New York, 1968) are both good textbook-like introductions, and George C. Vaillant's *Aztecs of Mexico: Origin, Rise, and Fall of the Aztec Nation*, rev. by Suzannah B. Vaillant (Garden City, 1962) is a well written and sound treatment. *The Handbook of South American Indians*, edited by Julian H. Steward, 7 vols. (Washington, D.C., 1946-59) is the standard reference work for the peoples of that area, while Julian H. Steward and Louis C. Faron's

Native Peoples of South America (New York, 1959) is a convenient and dependable textbook treatment. Sally Falk Moore's *Power and Property in Inca Peru* (Moringside Heights, 1958) is a careful, scholarly work treating not only landowning patterns but taxes, and law. *The Handbook of American Indians, North of Mexico*, edited by Frederick W. Hodge, 2 vols. (Washington, D.C., 1910; reprinted in New York, 1959) is basic for that area.

Harold E. Driver's *Indians of North America* (Chicago, 1962) is a standard systematic introduction with chapters on housing, crafts, property, kinship, and government, while Alvin M. Josephy's *The Indian Heritage of America* (New York, 1969) covers the same ground geographically, treating his subjects by tribal groupings. John W. Griffin, ed., *The Florida Indian and His Neighbors* (Winter Park, Florida, 1949) treats not only Florida Indians but those of the Caribbean and the southeastern United States as well and contains useful information. Almon W. Lauber, *Indian Slavery in Colonial Times Within the Present Limits of the United States* (New York, 1913) though old and disappointing, remains the most complete coverage of that subject. And Roy H. Pearce, *The Savages of America; A Study of the Indian and the Idea of Civilization* (Revised ed., Baltimore, 1965) is central to that question.

On land and labor problems in Latin America see W.W. Borah's brief but excellent *New Spain's Century of Depression* (Berkeley, 1951), François Chevalier, *Land and Society in Colonial Mexico; The Great Hacienda*, tr. by Alvin Eustis and edited by L.B. Simpson (Berkeley, 1963). L.B. Simpson himself has written two splendid works on *The Encomienda in New Spain; the Beginning of Spanish Mexico*, rev. ed., (Berkeley, 1950) and the *Exploitation of Land in Central Mexico in the Sixteenth Century* (Berkeley, 1952). A fascinating contemporary account full of information is Alonso de Zurita, *Life and Labor in Ancient Mexico; The Brief and Summary Relation of the Lords of New Spain*, tr. with introduction by Benjamin Keen (New Brunswick, 1964). The best places to begin for the Portuguese possessions in the New World are the works of Charles R. Boxer, principally his *Four Centuries of Portuguese Expansion, 1415-1825; A Succinct Survey* (Berkeley, 1969); *The Dutch Seaborne Empire, 1600-1800* (New York, 1965); *The Dutch in Brazil*, 1624-1654 (Oxford, 1957); and *The Golden Age of Brazil, 1695-1750; Growing Pains of a Colonial Society* (Berkeley,

1962). A.N. Marchant's *From Barter to Slavery; The Economic Relations of Portuguese and Indians in the Settlement of Brazil, 1500-1580* (Baltimore, 1942) remains excellent, and Caio Prado's *The Colonial Background of Modern Brazil*, tr. by Suzette Macedo (Berkeley, 1967) is a good interpretation. The Andean area has not received the attention that Mexico and Brazil have, but Donald L. Wiedner's "Forced Labor in Colonial Peru," *The Americas*, XVI (April, 1960), 357-383, deals with Indian labor, especially in mining and textile manufacture; James M. Lockhart, *Spanish Peru, 1532-1560; A Colonial Society* (Madison, 1968) has chapters on various groups in Spanish society in Peru, including encomenderos, merchants, artisans, Negroes and Indians; and John L. Phelan, *The Kingdom of Quito in the 17th Century; Bureaucratic Politics in the Spanish Empire* (Madison, 1967) has a chapter on textile mills and one on Indian labor.

Lewis Hanke recounts the debate that took place in Spain over the nature of the American Indians in his *Aristotle and the American Indians; A Study in Race Prejudice in the Modern World* (London, 1959) and S.A. Zavala explores *The Defense of Human Rights in Latin America, Sixteenth to Eighteenth Centuries* (Paris, 1964). Arthur Ramos's *The Negro in Brazil* (Washington, D.C., 1951) is good. C.R. Boxer wrote also on *Race Relations in the Portuguese Colonial Empire, 1415-1825* (Oxford, Eng., 1963), and Gilberto Freyre's *The Masters and the Slaves* (Casa-grande and Senzala); *A Study in the Development of Brazilian Civilization*, tr. by Samuel Putnam, 2d English-language ed., rev. (New York, 1956) is a provocative essay on the Negro as a formative influence in Brazilian civilization. Magnus Morner's *Race Mixture in the History of Latin America* (Boston, 1967) is a fine brief treatment of the problem. Fernando Romero's article "El negro en tierra firme durante el siglo XVI," *Actas y trabajos científicos del XXVII° Congreso Internacional de Americanistas*, II (Lima, 1939-42) argues that Negro slavery made possible the Spanish colonization of America. See also Roger Bastide, *African Civilizations in the New World*, tr. Peter Green (New York, 1971), Gonzales Aguirre Beltran, *La Poblacion Negra de Mexico*, 1519-1810 (Mexico City, 1946), Aguiles Escalante, *El Negro en Columbia* (Bogota, 1964), A. Arredondo, *El Negro en Cuba* (Habana, 1939), and James F. King, "The Negro in Continental Spanish America: A Select Bibliography." *Hispanic American Historical Review*, XXIV (1944), 547-559. Leo Wiener, *Africa and the Discovery of*

America, 3 vols. (Philadelphia, 1920-22), a curious work arguing that many crops, such as tobacco, supposed to have originated in the New World, actually were known in Africa before the discovery in North America, contains much interesting information but must be used with care.

Renaissance England's view of Africa and black Africans has been treated by Eldred D. Jones in two short books: *Othello's Countrymen; The African in English Renaissance Drama* (London, 1965) and *The Elizabethan Image of Africa* (Charlottesville, Va., 1971). Both are diffuse, repetitive, and lacking in synthetic analysis, but contain valuable information. The best description of the Atlantic slave trade remains Basil Davidson's *Black Mother; The Years of the African Slave Trade* (Boston, 1961) and a work of lesser weight covering the same subject is Daniel P. Mannix and Malcolm Cowley, *Black Cargoes; A History of the Atlantic Slave Trade, 1518-1865* (New York, 1962). Philip D. Curtin's excellent *Atlantic Slave Trade; A Census* (Madison, Wisc., 1969) is the best statistical analysis of the trade available. The central work of the Negro in Anglo-America is Winthrop D. Jordan, *White Over Black: American Attitudes Toward the Negro, 1550-1812* (Chapel Hill, N.C., 1968). There is no body of literature on seventeenth-century Anglo-American land and labor problems comparable to that for Mexico and Brazil, but Abbot E. Smith's *Colonists in Bondage; White Servitude and Convict Labor in America, 1607-1776* (Chapel Hill, N.C., 1947); Richard B. Morris's *Government and Labor in Early America* (New York, 1946); Wesley Frank Craven's *The Southern Colonies in the Seventeenth Century, 1607-1689* (Baton Rouge, La., 1949); and Carl Bridenbaugh's *Myths and Realities; Societies of The Colonial South* (Baton Rouge, La., 1952) are good starting places. Lewis C. Gray's *History of Agriculture in the Southern United States to 1860*, 2 vols. (Washington, D.C., 1933; reprinted in Gloucester, Mass., 1958) though old remains standard and sound.

The best one-volume history of the Negro in the Americas is John Hope Franklin's *From Slavery to Freedom; a History of Negro Americans* (New York, 3rd ed., 1966). Elso V. Goveia's *Slave Society in the British Leeward Islands at the End of the Eighteenth Century* (New Haven, Conn., 1965) is a detailed study of West Indian slavery, and Gaston Martin's *Histoire de l'esclavage dans les colonies francaises*

(Paris, 1948) does the same for the French areas. A convenient collection of excerpts from books and articles is Allen Weinstein and Frank Otto Gatell, eds., *American Negro Slavery; A Modern Reader* (New York, 1968). Ulrich B. Phillips' *American Negro Slavery; A Survey of the Supply, Employment and Control of Negro Labor as Determined by the Plantation Régime* (New York, 1918) is still the most comprehensive study of Anglo-American slavery, but it should be supplemented with Kenneth M. Stampp's *The Peculiar Institution: Slavery in the Ante-Bellum South* (New York, 1956). Several writers have offered challenging interpretations of special aspects of the slave society: Eugene D. Genovese, *The Political Economy of Slavery: Studies in the Economy and Society of the Slave South* (New York, 1964); Eric Eustace Williams, *Capitalism and Slavery* (New York, 1944); and Leon F. Litwack, *North of Slavery; The Negro in the Free States, 1790-1860* (Chicago, 1961) are examples. The debate over the economics of slavery is summarized by Harold D. Woodman, "The Profitability of Slavery: A Historical Perennial," *Journal of Southern History* (August, 1963).

The comparative history of slavery in the New World was started by Frank Tannenbaum in his *Slave and Citizen, The Negro in the Americas* (New York, 1947), a brief essay, in which he argued that Anglo-American slavery was uniquely harsh because it denied the slave status as a human being. Stanley M. Elkins in his *Slavery; a Problem in American Institutional and Intellectual Life* (Chicago, 1959) agreed, adding that Anglo-American slavery resulted from unrestricted capitalism and an impotent protestant church. Herbert S. Kelin pointed out in his *Slavery in the Americas; A Comparative Study of Virginia and Cuba* (Chicago, 1967) that Virginia developed a full-scale caste system that supported slavery while Cuba did not. These views were challenged, or at least put to serious question, by David B. Davis in his impressive *Problem of Slavery in Western Culture* already cited, by Arnold A. Sio's article "Interpretations of Slavery: The Slave Status in the Americas" in *Comparative Studies in Society and History* (April, 1965), and most recently by Carl N. Degler in *Neither Black nor White: Slavery and Race Relations in Brazil and the United States* (New York, 1971) who comes down hard with an argument that Latin American slavery was no less harsh than that in Anglo-America. A convenient collection of articles and excerpts on the question is Laura Foner and Eugene D. Genovese, eds., *Slavery in the New World; A Reader in Comparative History* (Englewood Cliffs, N.J., 1969).

Reverberations and Repercussions

The effects of European involvement in Africa during the slave trade during the slavery era are touched upon in a number of the works already cited, particularly Duffy's *Portuguese Africa*; Ajaya and Espie's *A Thousand Years of West African History*; Fage's *Introduction to the History of West Africa*; Blake's *Europeans in West Africa, 1450-1560*; Wyndham's *Atlantic and Slavery*; July's *History of the African People; and* Curtin's *Atlantic Slave Trade*, but the truth of the matter is that the problem has not been sufficiently investigated to allow a conclusive statement by anyone. The Luba and Lunda empires are treated by Jan Vansina in his *Kingdoms of the Savanna* (Madison, Wisc., 1968). For Dahomey Melville J. Herskovits' two-volume anthropological study *Dahomey, An Ancient West African Kingdom* (New York, 1938; reprinted Evanston, Ill., 1967) is basic. It might be supplemented by I.A. Akinjogbin, *Dahomey and its Neighbours, 1708-1818* (Cambridge, Eng., 1967), and C.W. Newbury, *The Western Slave Coast and Its Rulers* (Oxford, Eng., 1961). On the Ashanti see W.W. Claridge, *A History of the Gold Coast and Ashanti From the Earliest Times to the Commencement of the Twentieth Century*, 2 vols., 2nd ed. (London, 1964), Ivor Wilks, *The Northern Factor in Ashanti History* (Legon, 1961), R.S. Rattray, *Ashanti Law and Constitution* (Oxford, Eng., 1929), and Eva L.R. Meyerowitz, *Akan Traditions of Origin* (London, 1952), the latter to be used with care. Thomas Hodgkins's *Nigerian Perspectives* (London, 1960) is masterful for the whole of Nigerian history.

The best place to begin when considering repercussions in Europe of New World developments is with four lectures by John H. Elliott published as *The Old World and the New, 1492-1650* (Cambridge, Eng., 1970). Volume III of the *New Cambridge Modern History: The Counter-Reformation and Price Revolution, 1559-1610*, edited by R.B. Wernham, (Cambridge, Eng., 1968) will also prove useful. The first modern scholar to explore the vexing question of the effects of the opening of the Americas on Europe's economy was Earl J. Hamilton. In his *American Treasure and the Price Revolution in Spain, 1501-1650* (Cambridge, Mass., 1934) he argued that the influx of gold and silver from the New World provoked a price revolution that began in Spain and spread to the rest of Europe, inflating profits of merchants, encouraged capital formation as well as commercial and industrial growth, and long-range social changes. Objections to such a purely monetary explanation were raised by several writers; for a summary see John H. Elliott, *Imperial Spain, 1496-1716* (London, 1963), pp. 183-188. Works such as Fernand Braudel's *The Mediterranean and the Mediterranean World in the Age of Philip II*, second ed., tr. by S. Reynolds (New York, 1972) pointed out that much of the metal from the New World did not go into profit-making enterprizes or cause fundamental social change. It was not therefore the prime source of dynamic change in sixteenth-century Europe, as important as it was in sustaining price levels. Still other writers, notably Huguette and Pierre Chanu in their eight-volume study of *Seville et l'Atlantique 1504-1650* (Paris, 1955-59) and *L'Amerique et les Ameriques* (Paris, 1964) argued that the new American trade was more important in Europe's development than American gold and silver. Still others, such as John H. Elliott himself, have speculated that the myriad opportunities in all directions offered by the opening of the Americas was the key. The question, perhaps the most important and far-reaching in modern western history, thus remains unsettled.

The formation of an Atlantic civilization resulting from the opening of the Americas has long been recognized but little written about. Michael Kraus' *The Atlantic Civilization; Eighteenth Century Origins* (Ithaca, 1949; reissued 1966) is a pioneering work that falls short of the mark because it deals almost exclusively with the Anglo-Atlantic community. Robert O. Mead's *Atlantic Legacy; Essays in American-European Cultural History* (New York, 1969) carries the story to the present in somewhat broader context, but is still disappointing. Another effort worthy of more attention than it has received is Walter Prescott Webb's *The Great Frontier* (London, 1953), an attempt to apply the frontier thesis to European history. Webb saw the New World as Europe's frontier and the discovery as the opening of that frontier. A number of monographs detailing the assimilation of aspects of New

World developments into European culture have been produced; few, however, deal with Africa. Two of the latter deserve special mention: Pierre Verger, *Flux et Reflux de la traite des nègres entre le Golfe de Benin et Bahia de Todos os Santos du XVIIe au XIXe siècle* (Paris, 1968), and José Honorio Rodrigues, *Brazil and Africa*, tr. by Richard A. Mazzara and Sam Hileman (Berkeley, 1965). Both deal with continuing relations between Brazil and black Africa during and after the era of slavery.

The best account of the political struggles over ending the international slave trade is still W.E.B. Du Bois, *The Suppression of the African Slave Trade to the United States of America, 1638-1870* (New York, 1896). On western Africa during the nineteenth century see, in addition to titles already cited, C.D. Forde and P.M. Kaberry, ed., *West African Kingdoms in the Nineteenth Century* (London, 1967); Michael Crowder, *West Africa Under Colonial Rule* (London, 1968); and K.O. Dike, *Trade and Politics in the Niger Delta* (Oxford, Eng., 1956). Three brief but extremely useful works cover the United States' involvement in Africa: Peter Duignan and Clarence C. Clendenen, *The United States and the African Slave Trade, 1619-1862* (Stanford, 1963); C. Clendenen and P. Duignan, *Americans in Black Africa up to 1865* (Stanford, 1964); and C. Clendenen, Robert Collins, and P. Duignan, *Americans in Africa, 1865-1900* (Stanford, 1966). The role of missionaries in western Africa is detailed in J.F.A. Ajayi, *Christian Missions in Nigeria, 1841-1891* (London, 1965) and by E.A. Ayandele, *The Missionary Impact on Modern Nigeria, 1842-1914* (London, 1966), both nationalistic but thorough. Christopher Fyfe's *A History of Sierra Leone* (London, 1962) is the only thing available on that area. There is no satisfactory history of Liberia, though useful information can be found in C.H. Huberich, *The Political and Legislative History of Liberia*, 2 vols. (New York, 1947). Roland A. Oliver and Anthony Atmore, *Africa Since 1800* (London, 1967) is an excellent brief survey for the whole of Africa and has a good if short bibliography.

The literature on the origins and nature of racism is vast and varied. Of the theoretically oriented discussions Gordon Allport, *The Nature of Prejudice* (Cambridge, Mass., 1954) is sound and balanced. Dominique O. Mannoni, *Prospero and Caliban: The Psychology of Colonization*, trans. by Pamela Powesland (London, 1956), and E. Franklin Frazier, *Race and Culture Contacts in the Modern World* (New York,

1957) reflect valuable insights. Marvin Harris, *Patterns of Race in the Americas* (New York, 1964) is an excellent study of differing racial attitudes towards Indians and Negroes in the various areas of Latin America but of little use for Anglo-America. Two surveys of Anglo-American attitudes are Gunnar Myrdal *et al., An American Dilemma; The Negro Problem and Modern Democracy*, 2 vols., (New York, 1944) and a criticism of it by Herbert Aptheker, *The Negro People in America* (New York, 1946). Good special studies on Anglo-America are Thomas F. Gossett, *Race; The History of an Idea in America* (Dallas, 1963); William R. Stanton, *The Leopard's Spots: Scientific Attitudes Toward Race in America, 1815-59* (Chicago, 1960); and I.A. Newby, *Jim Crow's Defense; Anti-Negro Thought in America, 1900-1930* (Baton Rouge, 1965). Many of the works already cited deal with the problem in its historical settings, particularly David B. Davis's *The Problem of Slavery in Western Culture* and Winthrop D. Jordan's *White Over Black: American Attitudes Towards the Negro*. The Institute of Race Relations in London is putting out an interesting and useful series of studies of how attitudes towards race have evolved and functioned in various historical settings. Philip Mason has written several of the excellent studies, noteworthy among them his *Patterns of Dominance* (London, 1970) which treats racism in the context of European expansion, conquest and domination.

Index